U0506967
ANDY SUN
EXPLORE
THE
POWER

乡愁，是

一片白云 一汪清泉

一叶扁舟 一念相思

乡愁，是

打开尘封回忆的钥匙

游子心中柔软的惦念

乡 愁 · 中 国

Nostalgia of China

I

卷 壹

汉、英

《乡愁 · 中国》编委会　编

Edited by Editorial Board

李谨羽　译

Translated by Li Jinyu

北京出版集团公司

Beijing Publishing Group

北 京 出 版 社

Beijing Publishing House

《乡愁·中国》 编委会

Editorial Board of Nostalgia of China

前言

乡 愁， 是

一 片 白 云 一 汪 清 泉

一 叶 扁 舟 一 念 相 思

乡 愁， 是

打 开 尘 封 回 忆 的 钥 匙

游 子 心 中 柔 软 的 惦 念

乡愁—— 2013 年中央城镇化工作会议后风靡全国的一个词语。据统计，2013 年全国流动人口 2.45 亿，其中 80% 来自农村，保守估计，每 3 个农民里就有 1 个离开农村。在这场城镇化建设中，我们不禁要问：我们要创造什么？又要留下什么？在这一点上，习近平总书记给了我们明确的要求，他提出城镇化建设要让城市融入大自然，让居民望得见山、看得见水、记得住乡愁。这既是要求，也是一种担忧，值得每一位爱家、爱国人士关切。

费孝通先生在其作品《乡土中国》中不禁感慨，城镇化建设会不会使我们的乡土本色退化，会不会割断乡村的历史文脉？正是基于“分享乡情，留下乡念，感受乡愁”这一宗旨，我们编写出版了《乡愁·中国》（共 10 卷），通过对以“乡愁”为主题的图片展示与文字记录，突显处于历史转型期的中国百姓对往日山水乡景的丝丝怀念，对家乡祖国的浓浓眷恋；通过文化舆论引导，引起全社会对中国传统村落存留状态、生态文明的关注，并使得中国民风习俗中的优良传统得以延续，进而达到农村城镇化保护与发展共赢的目的。

为了面向全社会收集有关“乡愁”主题的图文内容，我们组织了“乡愁·中国”主题征稿大赛，并由著名摄影家解海龙、于云天、段岳衡等人组成评委会。此次大赛通过网络、杂志等多渠道面向全社会海选，初步征集一部分优秀的关于“乡愁”的图文作品，并从中选拔出50位优秀选手。在经过关于中国传统村落文化的统一培训后，50位优秀选手被派往指定的传统村落观察、体验、拍摄7~15天，每人提交调查报告及拍摄图片。最终，选手们的优秀图文资料被精编成为本套10卷图书。

本次所选村落几乎全是经国家文物局等相关机构认定的最具中国特色、最具乡愁气息的传统村落。全套书共含100个传统村落，按照100个村落日出时间的先后顺序划分成10卷。所有图片均由选手实地拍摄，文字均为选手根据调查、采访、收集到的资料整理撰写而成。每个村落都将突出其作为中国传统村落之美，以及其被保护的核心特征。每一个村落的摄影作品都会涵盖整体面貌、特色建筑、人与村落、手工遗迹、历史遗存五大主题，为了获取这些作品，很多地方不惜动用了航拍设备，只为能让读者以最全面的视角去解读村落，品味乡愁。

乡愁，是一首无法言说的诗，是一幅不可描摹的画；乡愁，是一种无法回归的寻找，是一生都不可停止的守望。在城镇化进程中，越来越多的人离开美丽的乡村，走进现代化的城市，越来越多的古村落、老建筑、老手艺在逐渐消失。原本我们习以为常、嬉戏打闹的村庄成为被保护的对象，而故乡也慢慢成为再也回不去的回忆。

我们愿本套书的出版不仅能唤起您的回忆，更能激起您的思考与行动。

记住乡愁，是每一位中国人的使命。
守护乡愁，是每一位中国人的责任。

让我们用城市规划师周晓影的一段文字，开启对本书的阅读吧：

我家门口有一棵五六十年的梧桐树，春天闻着满树花香，夏天在树下荡着秋千听蝉鸣。不远处，有一个池塘，池塘里小鱼游来游去，池塘边有一块早年留下来的石磨盘，我在那里和小伙伴过家家、捉知了……

编委会

2016.2.1

Preface

Nostalgia, aroused by
A white cloud
A clear spring

A small rowboat
Or the sentiment
of yearning;

Nostalgia has become a buzzword across China since the 2013 Central Conference on Urbanization. Statistics show that the number of the floating population in China was 245 million in 2013 and 80% of them were from rural areas. It is safe to say that one in three peasants have left the countryside. Faced with this unprecedented revolutionary urbanization, we cannot but ask ourselves: what do we want to make and what do we want to keep? In this regard, President Xi Jinping has explicitly demanded that urbanization aims to integrate cities with nature so as to enable residents to enjoy the landscape and remember their roots. It's not only a demand but also a worry that deserves the concern of whoever loves their homes and country.

In the book *From the Soil*, Mr. Fei Xiaotong has proposed a question that whether the urbanization will erode the true colors of the countryside and cut off its culture traditions. For the purposes of sharing, keeping and feeling the nostalgia, we have compiled and published a series of 10 volumes under the name *Nostalgia of China.* We want to emphasize how ordinary Chinese people miss the rural landscape from the past and love their home country during this historical transformation period via pictures and essays themed around a sense of nostalgia. We also intend to, by guiding public opinion, draw the attention of the whole society to the preservation of traditional villages in China and their ecological culture so as to pass down the fine fol customs and achieve a win-win outcome between development and conservation through rural urbanization.

In order to collect nostalgia-themed materials from th whole society, we organized the Nostalgia of China Essay Competition and selected the top 50 authors through maga zines and internet media like MicroBlog, which was judged a panel of renowned photographers such as Xie Hailong, Y Yuntian and Duan Yueheng. After a unified training session on the culture of traditional villages in China, these authors were sent to assigned villages and stayed for 7 to 15 days t observe first-hand gaining personal experience and shoot photos before submitting individual reports and correspon ing photos; all of which were used to compile these 10 volumes.

These selected villages are the most nostalgia provoking communities with the most Chinese characteristics recognized by organs as the State Administration of Cultur Heritage. The series cover a total of 100 traditional village which are categorized into 10 volumes, in the sequence ac-

Nostalgia is
The key
to dust-laden
memories

And

always
on the mind of
those traveling
afar.

ording to when dawn breaks. All the photos within are taken rst-hand and all the essays are composed by the authors rough investigations, interviews and collection. Highlighted each village's beauty as a traditional village and its core eatures that needs to be conserved. Each of the village is hotographically presented through five aspects: overview, haracteristic architecture, villagers and the village itself, andicrafts and historical relics. In many cases, aerial hotography was used so as to give the readers a comprehensive view of the village as well as a better taste of the ostalgia that comes along with it.

Nostalgia is an unspoken verse, an uncopiable painting, quest with no coming back, and a vigil with no end. On the ay of urbanization, an increasing number of people are aving their beautiful home villages for modern cities, but ore and more ancient villages, buildings and craftsmanship e disappearing. Villages where we used to live and play are ut under protection, and hometowns are fading into inaccessible memories.

We do hope that upon the publishing of this series, we ould not only help you recall your memories, but also movate you to think and act. It is a mission for every Chinese to keep nostalgia in mind and a responsibility to guard that nostalgia.

Now, let's start the book with a paragraph beautifully written by a city planner Zhou Xiaoying below.

"A sycamore tree in its fifties or sixties stands before our house. It sends forth a delicate fragrance in the spring and provides shelter for us to play on a swing and enjoy the chirping of cicadas in the summer. There's a pond not far away from it, where little fish swim freely. Beside the pond, an ancient millstone rendered a perfect place for me and the fellas to play the house game or catch cicadas..."

Editorial Board
Feb. 1, 2016

100

村落经纬度坐标图

Geographic coordinate graph of the villages

经纬度
是影响日出时间的一个因素

Geographic coordinates partly determines when the sun rises in the villages

采用 2°×2° 网格法，将经纬线 16°N ~ 54°N、72°E ~ 136°E（中国在内）区域共分成 19×32 个网格单元，分别标出 100 个村落的经纬度位置

The horizontal axis ranges from 72°E to 136°E while the vertical axis from 16°N to 54°N, covering mainland China. Divided by every 2°, the graph consists of 19x32 grids where the 100 villages are pinned accordingly

48° N

40° N

32° N

24° N

80° E

88° E

96°

I 28°N ~ 50°N, 121°E ~ 127°E

II 25°N ~ 31°N, 119°E ~ 121°E

III 26°N ~ 40°N, 118°E ~ 119°E

IV 25°N ~ 30°N, 117°E ~ 118°E

V 24°N ~ 36°N, 117°E

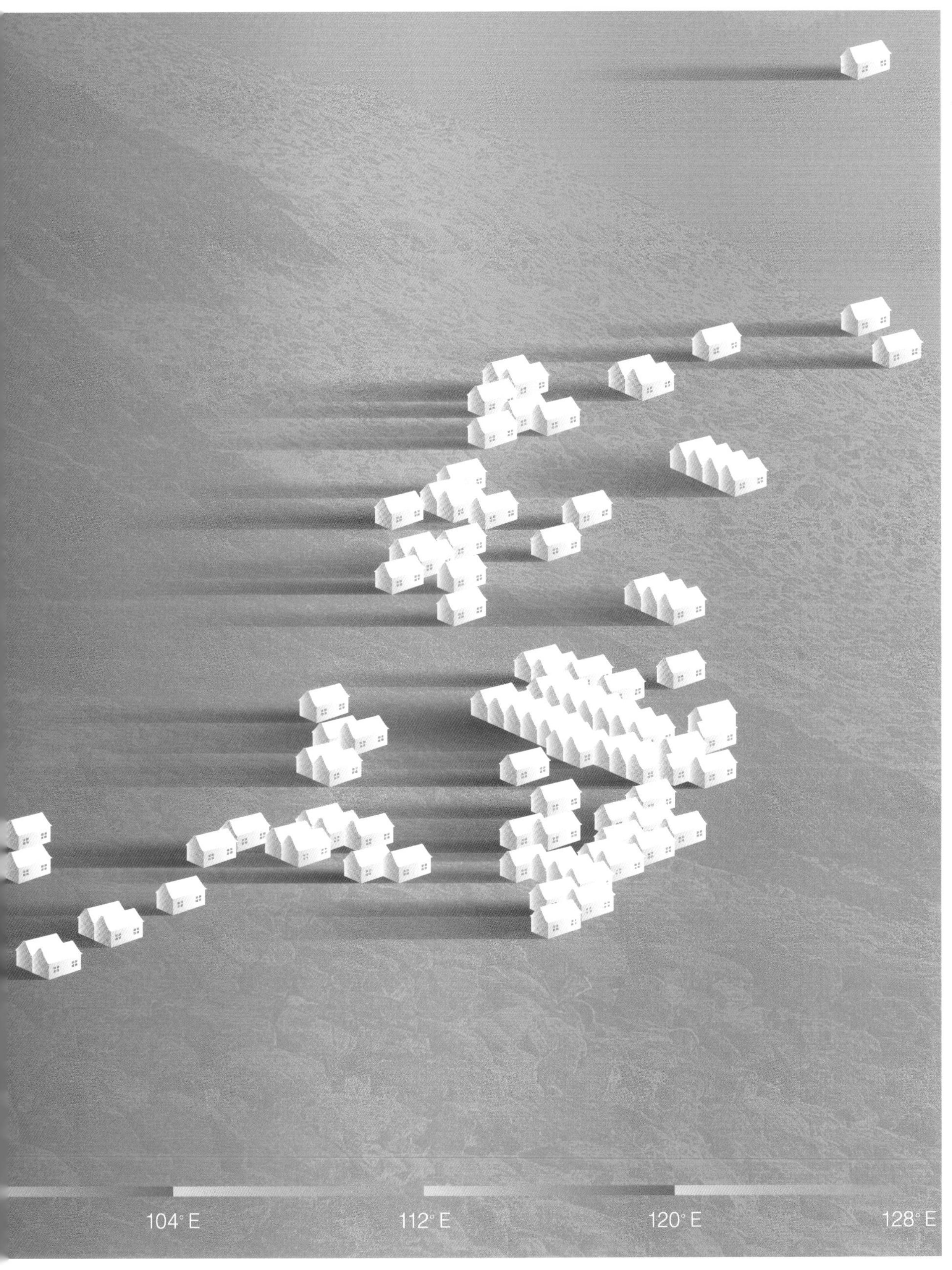

VI 24°N ~ 39°N, 115°E ~ 117°E

VII 25°N ~ 40°N, 113°E ~ 115°E

VIII 25°N ~ 36°N, 110°E ~ 113°E

IX 25°N ~ 30°N, 108°E ~ 110°E

X 22°N ~ 48°N, 87°E ~ 106°E

卷 壹

28°N ~
50°N,
121°E ~
127°E

48°

40°

32°

24°

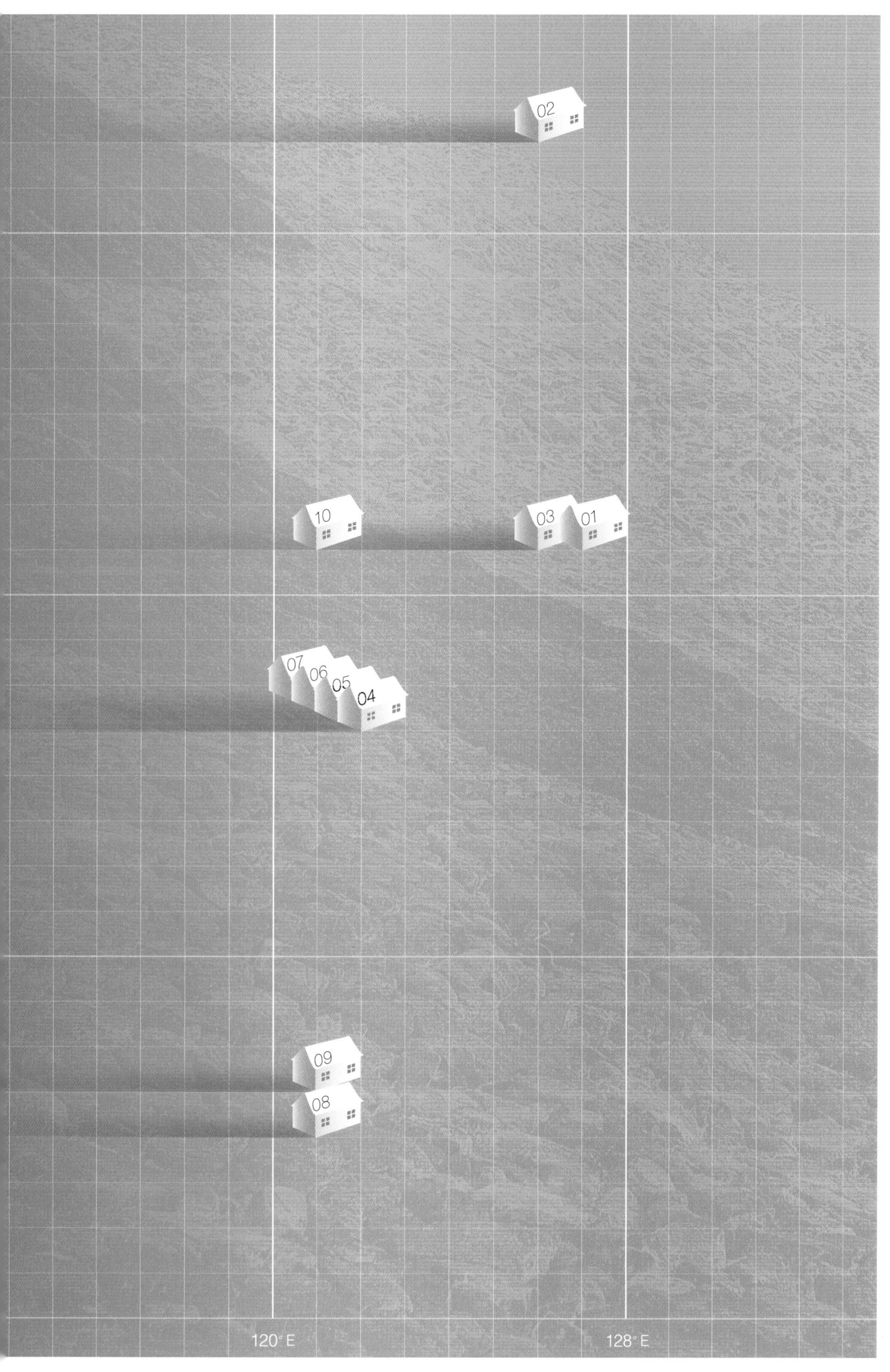
02
10
03
01
07
06
05
04
09
08
120° E
128° E

01

锦江木屋村

调查报告原文 / 摄影
王彬
Reported / photograghed by
Wang Bin

> 为更好地保存木屋原貌，修缮过程中，工匠们不会改变木屋的位置和面积

The locations and areas of cabins remained unchanged during the renovation so as to better preserve them in their original state

白山深处掩柴扉

长白山深处古木参天，在苍松、白桦、蓝天的映衬下，一条蜿蜒的林中小路通向一个山谷。20 多人家错落有致地分布在朝阳的山坡上，四周原始森林与人工森林、次生林杂处，村外有锦江流过。木木瓦、木烟囱、木栅栏、木柴垛……整个村庄见不到一块砖瓦，这就是吉林省抚松县漫江镇锦江木村——一座完全由原木建造的村子，被誉为长白山最后的木屋村落。

根据抚松县史志记载，锦江木屋村始建于 1937 年，至今有 70 多年的历史，现存 50 余座原生态木这些木屋原名孤顶子，以当地一座孤立突出的山峰命名。20 世纪 90 年代中期，通化师范学院美术系位教授在长白山老林子里写生时，发现了这些木屋建筑群。于是，这座藏于深山的村子就展现在世人面吸引着一些专家学者、艺术家纷纷前往考察、采风。后因为此村靠近锦江，被人们称为锦江木屋村。

纵横上千千米的长白山区是多民族融合的舞台，早在三四千年以前，这里就有人类生息的印迹。

省抚松县是满族发祥地之一，清康熙、乾隆时期为保护这块“龙兴之地”将之封禁长达 200 年，直到光绪年间才解禁。解禁后，关内大批农民蜂拥而至，聚居而成村。他们藏身密林深处，外界联系甚少，依靠着无穷无尽的森林资源生活。

这里的山民们延续了满族先民的居住习俗，砍树造屋。其建造工艺在清朝时期已经相当熟，当地人称之为木克楞，意为用原木凿刻，垒垛建屋，如同上下门牙咬合一样；也有人称之霸王圈，意喻房子非常牢固，即使骁勇的霸王也对它无可奈何。建筑学上称之为井干式房屋，其形似用原木围成的井口护栏之意。

木克楞房子有四大优点：一是就地取材，山民上山寻找树木，运下山来即可锯为窗、瓦、；二是加工粗放，建屋的木头不锯不雕，甚至连树皮也无须剥掉；三是保暖防风，原木加泥

^工匠们把
木头有序地
叠压起来

A craftsman
lays the logs
in an orderly
fashion

的墙壁厚度可达 1/3 米，还有火炕取暖，足以抵御北方严寒；四是耐用，松木油分高，潮、耐腐蚀，可经百年风雪而不朽。如果墙壁倾斜，重新翻盖即可再用。尤其是大封山时节，村民烧起火炕，把一根完整的倒木（因自然因素折断的完整树木，非人砍伐）掏空竖立在屋外做成烟囱，屋内暖意融融，成为连皇帝也艳羡的养生别墅。年乾隆东巡时，见到长白山区的木克楞和满语称之为呼兰的烟囱，赋诗赞道："木烟囱犹故俗，纸窗日影正新嘉。盆中更有仙家草，五叶朱旒拙四桠。"诗中描绘了这一幅美景：晨光映红了白雪，山里一户农家的木烟囱里炊烟袅袅，新糊的纸窗格外亮，窗台上的花盆中栽有一棵"关东三宝"之首的人参，四品叶的枝丫、五个瓣的参叶、红色的参子相互辉映，把这山居装点得绚丽多彩……

锦江木屋群修建时，正值日占时期，日军对此地实行并村管理，将几个村合并一起，形成了现在聚居的村落。到 20 世纪 90 年代，这里已有百余户人家。之后，于木材数量减少、价格上涨，以及交通不便等原因，一些木屋已无法维持下去。在地政府的支持下，约有 2/3 的村民迁离木屋村。剩余的木屋经过主人的维修改造，成为人们旅游、摄影的好去处。这些原木垒砌的木屋如同一件件木雕艺术品：新抹涂的墙在绿树丛中鲜亮，木瓦因氧化而呈青灰色，背坡的木瓦则长满嫩绿的青苔；烟囱高过屋顶，有的上面长满云芝与"老牛肝"，缕缕炊烟散发着木头燃烧的芳香；檐下悬挂着黄黄的玉米、红红的辣椒，庭院里、房顶上晾晒着蘑菇、五味子、烟叶……些有木瓦的房舍分外显眼，有的金黄，有的灰白，年久的则变成了黑色，在黑沉沉树木衬托下，质朴醇厚，像长白山人的个性。如果冬日来访，则又是一番景象：皑白雪覆盖着五彩斑斓的木屋，家家户户的门上、仓上贴着大红的对联，还有彩色的签、院门口高挂的红灯……随着知名度的提高，这深山的小村也有了迁入者。几个地的姑娘远嫁这里，跟木屋相守，与山泉做伴。这些年轻女子把木屋收拾得干净洁，在院子里晾晒着人参、蘑菇等山货，生活十分富足。小伙子们负责早出晚归"跑"，他们结伴进山挖"棒槌"（人参）、打松子，在大山里，树丛中，到处寻宝：榛子、萄、五味子、地龙骨、天麻，还有野菜——大叶芹、刺嫩芽、薇菜、木耳、榆黄蘑……些山珍不但自家吃，更主要的是卖给城里人。村里"木屋人家"的主人老邹就是这一位勤劳致富的村民。复员的他回来至今没离开过这个村子。2013 年他带领部分民成立了金源木屋旅游合作社，这也是村子里第一个经营实体，生意做得红红火火。的妻子还在家里开了一个小卖店，大女儿现在上海工作，小儿子在家里和他一起经合作社，儿媳妇巧手剪的窗花在这一带小有名气，现在她正计划着把剪窗花做成屋村旅游文化的又一个品牌。

按道理说老邹现在应该满足了。然而他总会透出一丝担心和惆怅：外来的商人在木屋改造中嗅到了商机，生态环境会不会被破坏？2千米外的锦江还能不能保护住其清凌凌的水源？木屋过去一直用木瓦防水，近几年来木瓦却被蓝色的塑料布取代，就连冬季保温、栽种人参等也用塑料布。经济效益虽提高了，但古朴的农家院落却变得不伦不类。

当然，也有一些当地人对旅游开发充满憧憬。木工老陈凭一身传统手艺，带领几位施工人员对这片区域进行翻新改造。只要这里不断进行建设，他就一直有活干，有收益。

木屋是不可再生的满族文化资源，是人、山、林、水和谐共生的见证。藏在深山里与世无争的村民们忽然成了镜头下的主角，采集打猎的生活方式受到商品经济的冲击。当地人能不能经受住这样的考验？作为游客，千里迢迢来到这深山老林中寻访，不但能体验到久违的自然野趣，还可以用镜头记录下一段正在变化的历史……

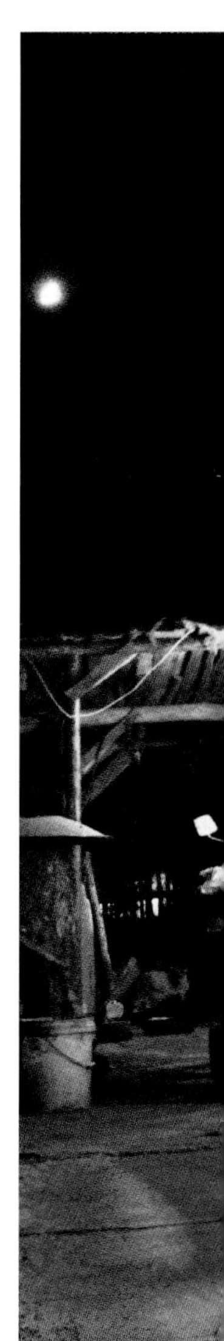

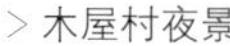

> 木屋村夜景

The village by night

一帆風順
水順人意
好景好前程

Jinjiang Cabin Village

Deep in the Changbai Mountains, a trail under skyscraping pines and birches winds its way to a valley where around two dozen households scatter in picturesque disorder over the sun-facing hillside. The village, located next to Jinjiang (Jin River), is surrounded by the intermingling of primary, secondary and artificial forests. Not a single tile can be seen in the whole village and all is wooden: walls, shingles, chimneys, fences, woodpiles, etc. This is Jinjiang Cabin Village, an utterly log-built village that is honored as "the Last Log Cabin Village in the Changbai Mountains", in Manjiang Town, Fusong County, Jilin Province.

According to the annals of Fusong County, the village was established in 1937. After over 70 years, there are more than 50 primitive cabins left standing. It was once named "Gudingzi"due to the prominence of an isolated peak in the local area. In the middle of the 1990s, an art professor from Tonghua Normal University ran into this group of cabins when coming to the forests to paint from nature, and regarded it as a living fossil embodying the log culture in the Changbai Mountains because of the absence of bricks, tiles or even plastic sheets. After that, this village hidden behind the mountains was revealed to the world. In recent years, waves of scholars and artists visited the village for observation and collection purposes. Later, it was called Jinjiang Village because of the adjacent Jin River and now it is known as Jinjiang Cabin Village among tourists.

The Changbai Mountain Range which stretches thousands of miles has been a stage for multiple ethnic groups to live, multiply and integrate as early as three or four millennia ago. The range represents the birthplace of the Manchus and was put under protection as the birthplace of dragons and blocked by the Qing Emperors Kangxi and Qianlong for more than 200 years. When the blockade was lifted by Emperor Guangxu, peasants inside the Shanhaiguan Pass got outside and flocked here as woodcutters, reclaimers, gold miners, ginseng pickers and huntsmen. They built log cabins to keep out the cold in deep forests, where some habitable spots became more and more densely populated and thus evolved into villages. These remote villages had very few connections with the outside world and villagers lived on the inexhaustible resources.

^锦江与漫江交汇处

The junction of the Jin and Man Rivers

The villagers lived in log cabins just as their Manchu ancestors did. Construction skills of such cabins were already very well developed in the Qing Dynasty and they were constructed in an architecturally sophisticated structure: laying logs horizontally one on top of each other and overlapping them at interlocking corners. These cabins were called by the locals as "*Mukeleng*", meaning that the round logs were hewn and stacked as strong as clenching teeth. They were also called "*Bawangquan*" (the Conqueror's Circle), indicating that they were so impregnable that even someone as valiant as the Conqueror could do nothing about it.

Mukeleng had four merits. Firstly, they drew on local resources as trees were abundant there and downed logs could be easily found, transported and made into chimneys, shingles and walls. Secondly, the logs were processed in an extensive manner without sawing or carving or even barking, thus saving both time and labor. Thirdly, they were insulated and windproof. The 0.33-*meter*-thick log-mud-mixed walls plus kang (heated brick beds) were more than enough to keep out the bitter cold in the north. Lastly, they were durable. The ample amount of oil in pine ensured its resistance to moisture, corrosion and rot even after exposure to blizzards for hundreds of years. If the walls got sloped, some renovation would fix them.

Especially when heavy snow cut off the mountain passes, villagers would heat their kang and erect a hollowed out log outside the cabin as "*Hulan*" (chimney in the Manchu language), making their home into a cosy villa that even an emperor would be eager to have. Emperor Qianlong was deeply impressed by the sight of *Mukeleng* and *Hulan* during his eastern inspection tour and poeticized the scene as follows: "the early morning sunlight fell upon the snow and shone upon the new paper windows of a rural household, from whose chimney smoke spiralled. A ginseng plant, top of the three treasures in Northeast China, grew in a pot on the windowsill. The ginseng was at its prime with four leaves, each of which was comprised of five leaflets, and plenty of showy red berries, adding colour to the cabin."

The cabins were constructed at a time when Japanese invaders occupied the area and merged villages for the convenience of governance. That was how the current compact communities first came into being. There were over a hundred households living there in the 1990s. Afterwards, some cabins were out of repair for many years due to the decrease in the amount of timber, the increase in timber price and inconvenient transportation, as thus, were no longer safe to live in. Around two thirds of villagers moved away from their cabins under the support of the government. The remaining ones maintained and renovated their cabins and the village has become an attractive destination for tourists and photographers. These log-stacked cabins are nothing less than works of art. Freshly mud-smeared walls shine brightly against the backdrop of greenery. Some shingles have faded into steel grey due to oxidation while their counterparts in the shady areas of the hillside are crawling with dense green clumps of moss. Smoke curls up from chimneys that rise above rooftops, and you can smell the fragrance of new wood burning. Some of the chimneys are covered with turkey tail mushrooms and "artist's conk". There are yellow corns and red peppers hanging from the eaves, and mushrooms, five-flavour berries and yellow tobacco being sun-cured in courtyards and on rooftops. Cabins with shingles, whether golden or greyish white orange-blackened, stand out against the dark silhouette of the trees, plain and mellow, just like the people living in the Changbai Mountains. If visited on a winter's day, the village would be a snow-white world dotted with colourful cabins: red couplets, multi-coloured decorations, red lanterns, etc.

The increasingly famous village has welcomed a few migrants despite its remoteness. Those migrants are girls who married to villagers here and moved from their far-away homes to cabins near mountain springs. These literate and stylish young girls keep their cabins nice and neat and dry ginseng, mushrooms and other forest products in their courtyards under the sun, living a life of prosperity. Men go out early into the mountains looking for treasures from nature, such as hazels, grapes, five-flavour berries, Japanese yams, Gastrodia elata and wild vegetables like Ostericum sieboldii, Aralia elata, Osmunda japonica, Auricunlaria auricula and golden oyster mushrooms, and they don't come back till dusk. Some end up on their dinner tables, but the majority are sold to city dwellers. Autumn is a season for even more harvests. Villagers go into the mountain in groups for ginseng and pine nuts. They carry baskets with them no matter what. Their hard work really pays off and they have very decent annual incomes.

Mr. Zou, owner of Muwu Renjia (Log Cabin Household), which is a hostel in the village, is one of those who have become better off through hard work. He came back to the village after his demobilization and stayed. In 2013, Jinyuan Cabin Tourism Cooperative was founded under his leadership. It is the first operational entity in the village and his integrity and enthusiasm make it a booming one. His wife is running a grocery, his daughter working in Shanghai, and his son assisting him with the management of the cooperative. His daughter-in-law is starting to gain local publicity for her craft of paper-cutting pasted on panes and making efforts to turn it into another brand in the village's tourism culture.

Mr. Zou should logically be rather content now. However, he's still somewhat worried about whether the ecological environment will be ruined and if the Jin River, their mother river lying just two *kilometres* away, might not remain crystal clear if outsiders sensed the business opportunities in cabin transformation. People have been substituting blue plastic sheets for shingles that were traditionally used for water tightness. They even use those plastic sheets for heat preservation in winters and ginseng plantation. While it brings obvious economic benefits, it also imposes something unfit for a village of primitive simplicity.

Of course, some local people are totally looking forward to tourism development. One of them is Mr. Chen who knows many traditional crafts. He is leading several builders to renovate and refurbish cabins in the area. As long as construction work is on, he will always have a job and a stable source of income.

Log cabins represent a non-renewable source of Manchu culture as well as a witness to the harmonious coexistence of humanity, mountains, forests and waters. Villagers that held themselves aloof from the world in the deep mountains are suddenly in the spotlight. Their traditional lifestyles of collecting and hunting come under attack of the commodity economy. Are the locals able to go through such a test? Tourists that come a long way to this village not only get to experience the fun of natural wildness that is long-lost to them, but also record a history of transformation via their camera lens.

< 未完工的木屋顶结构

A roof under construction

^ 宁静的小院

A tranquil yard

∨ 木屋内的陈设——
这是最典型的中国东北
农村人家生活的素描

The interior display of a cabin, the epitome of rural life in northeast China

< 客栈的房前屋后挂满了农具，显示出当地人纯朴、简单的生活方式

Around the inns hang a variety of farm tools, manifesting a self-evident lifestyle of simplicity and honesty

∧客栈的房前屋后挂满了农具，显示出当地人纯朴、简单的生活方式

Around the inns hang a variety of farm tools, manifesting a self-evident lifestyle of simplicity and honesty

∧有的木屋已被改造成客栈，迎接八方来客

Some cabin have been transformed into inns that welcome tourists from all over the world

02

新生村

调查报告原文 / 摄影
关秀峰

Reported / photograghed by
Guan Xiufeng

> 如今政策好了，生活水平提高了，政府为家家盖起了砖、石、水泥结构的住房，屋内宽敞明亮，既有当年游猎时居住的房屋风格，又有现代别墅的感觉

Thanks to favorable policies, the living standards have improved and the government has built houses with bricks, stones and concrete for all local families. The interiors of which are bright. The houses combine the traditional style of the original nomadic life and the modern villa style as well

高高的兴安岭，一片大森林，森林里住着勇敢的鄂伦春，一呀一匹烈马、一呀一杆枪，獐狍野鹿满遍野，打也打不尽……

这首人们耳熟能详的歌曲，形象地描绘出了鄂伦春人的狩猎生活。鄂伦春人自古生活在黑龙江流的深山密林之中，被誉为兴安岭上的猎神。因为与山水丛林、野兽鱼鸟为伴，鄂伦春人相信万物有灵、人合一。他们信奉萨满教，日、月、风、雷、山、水都是他们崇拜的对象。萨满意指人与神灵之间的使是鄂伦春人生产生活中的祈求与希冀，在遭遇恶劣天气或重大疾病时，他们都会祈求萨满施展巫术除灾难。

“一载浪荡不回家，自有穹庐障风雨”生动地描绘了鄂伦春人曾经粗犷豪放的生活。1953 年，游于黑龙江省爱辉县境内的十几个部落的上百名鄂伦春同胞，在政府安排下结束了“桦皮为屋、兽皮为

肉为食”的原始游猎生活，定居于小兴安岭东麓的刺尔滨河畔，从而由原始氏族社会末期一进入社会主义时期，这就是黑河市爱辉区新生鄂伦春族自治乡新生村。经过学习和锻炼，他使惯了猎枪的手握起拖拉机的方向盘也同样灵活，过去虽习惯于采集山野菜，但现在也能娴地侍弄地里的庄稼。历史掀开了新的一页，村庄取名为新生，即是此意。

新生村是乡政府所在地，交通便利，环境优美，土地肥沃，四季皆景：春看杜鹃红艳似火，望绿海浩瀚无垠，秋观漫山红叶片片，冬赏冰雪玉树琼枝。全村有鄂伦春族 60 多户，人口不 200 人。由于与汉族通婚，一部分鄂伦春人已被同化。在长期的狩猎生活中，鄂伦春人创造独特的衣、食、住、行文化和萨满文化，丰富的动植物资源是新生村鄂伦春文化得以延续的基础，生村被誉为北方游猎第一乡。

虽然过上了相对现代的生活，但村民仍习惯身着鄂伦春传统服饰，房前屋后也装饰着各种民族特色的兽皮制品、桦皮制品、骨制品、编织品等手工艺品，游客还可以现场观看和体验手工艺品的制作过程。

当年鄂伦春人刚下山定居时，条件简陋。住房是用木桦子（大块的劈柴）和泥砌成，房顶用小叶章草苫盖。后来陆续改建了新的砖瓦房，屋檐、屋脊被装饰成传统木屋帐篷的样子。屋内有线电视、移动电话、自来水等设施一应俱全，富裕的人家还添了轿车。走进村民家，仓房里的大豆满满当当，院子里的芸豆更是堆得跟小山一样。

在新生村，游客可以品尝野味，可以坐上桦皮船在呼玛河上漂流，或骑马射箭、河边垂钓。夜晚，伴着鄂伦春族姑娘们的轻歌曼舞，游客可以一起狂欢，欢乐的气氛达到高潮，一天的疲惫都烟消云散。

在这里还可以看到鄂伦春族的传统住所——仙人柱，它类似美洲印第安人的庐帐，是因鄂伦春人游猎生活而产生的栖身之地。仙人柱利用松木或桦木做支架，围上桦树皮，冬季则换兽皮围盖，其底部直径七八米，高五六米，顶端露出空隙用来出烟和采光。地中间生篝火，可做饭、取暖和照明。仙人柱附近往往有个桦树皮搭建的仓库，将猎获到的食物放在上面储存起来，鄂伦春语称之为奥伦。夜晚，老人们便围坐在篝火旁给孩子们讲神话故事，猎人们围着篝火跳起欢快的斗熊舞，表达对火神的敬仰。鄂伦春人崇拜山神白那恰，他们会把心中白那恰的形象画在距离地面两米左右裸露的树干上，并用红布遮盖着，这又给树林增添了原始感和神秘感。过去每当猎人们打红围（即打虎、熊等大型猛兽）前都要祭拜山神，求其保佑他们收获猎物并平安归来。

鄂伦春人热爱大森林，对林木有着特殊的感情。由于对山路熟、善骑马，他们成为外人进入森林的向导。新生村还有一支护林马队，他们坚持巡山、护林，打击盗猎、盗伐，甚至深山追逃、禁毒。春夏蚊虫蛇蚁叮咬，秋冬风刀霜剑肆虐，四季经常有黑熊、野猪等凶猛野兽出没，可以说危险无处不在。若遇“哟——嗬”，一声悠扬高亢的吆喝，一群肤色黝黑、细眼高颧、端坐马背、身背钢枪的鄂伦春人在密林中疾驰而过，那就是护林马队的身影。虽已告别打猎生活，但是千年传承下来的民族文化和英雄情怀并没有消失。

鄂伦春人的礼节很多：在猎场或途中，遇到长辈要立即下马站在路旁，等其走过方可上马；客人来到，男主人要热情欢迎，并膝请安，妇女要用双手贴在前额上深深地鞠躬，然后将客人让进屋；招待客人吃饭要拿出家里最好的食品，第一道饮食是奶茶，主菜以肉食为主。

莽莽兴安岭栖息着鹿、狍、野猪、熊等野生动物，纵横交错的河流潜游着各种鱼类，这是鄂伦春人的衣食之源。狩猎、捕鱼是男人的工作，他们用铁叉捕获细鳞鱼、哲罗鱼、大马哈鱼等，放上野葱、柳蒿芽炖着吃，味道相当鲜美。鄂伦春妇女擅长制作皮毛和桦皮制品，桦树皮具有防腐、防蚀、不易变形的特点。在五六月份的时候，她们扒下

^秋天到了，为了冬天牲畜过冬的饲料，鄂伦春农民不停地往家运送牧草，为的是自家的牲畜能吃饱，安全越冬

Autumn is here. The Oroqen farmers are carrying pastures back home to store feed for their livestock in winter

桦树皮，将桦树皮加工成盛水盛奶的桦皮桶，装饭带菜的桦皮篓，装烟叶的桦皮烟盒、桦皮针线盒等，不但实用，而且做工精细，外形美观。桦树皮还能做成船只（鄂伦春语叫木莫沁），既轻便又结实，一个人就能扛起一只船，而承载的重量却能达到四五百斤。

在漫长的游猎生活期里兽皮是做衣服的主要材料。鄂伦春妇女能将不同季节打猎所得的兽皮，根据其部位和特点缝制成衣裤、靴帽、被褥、睡袋等，甚至连边角料也能做成漂亮的皮兜、香囊、荷包、腰带和猎刀的佩饰等。新生村的孟兰杰就是鄂伦春族狍皮制作技艺国家级非物质文化遗产传承人。独具特色的狍皮服饰还留存着当初的温暖，而对于文化传统的铭记和传承则成为鄂伦春人心中的惦念和寄托。

每年 8 月 6 日是鄂伦春族特有的古伦木沓节。游客可以在这天深深感受到鄂伦春人的热情：上马酒、下马酒让人盛情难却；少女敬献花环、载歌载舞让人目不暇接。每年第一场雪后上山狩猎仍是惯例，不过现如今大家都是开着货车上山，再用车满载战利品回来，效率更高、更便捷。

鄂伦春族在莽莽兴安岭上生息繁衍、变迁融合，到如今的鄂伦春人，有变又有不变。不变的是他们仍生存在这里，骨子里延续着古老的习俗，继承着前人的精神传统；变的是他们的眼界越来越宽、腰包越来越鼓、生活方式越来越时尚。在走出山林 60 多年后，鄂伦春人和他们的新生村已经成为一个传统和现代文明交融演变的标本。

^初秋，眼前是白色的白桦林，随着目光的延伸，一个村落展现在眼前

Early autumn. Right in front of our eyes are the white birch forests. In the distance, we see a small village

Xinsheng Village

"In the high Lesser Khingan Range covered by forests, lived the brave Oroqen people. Equipped with horses and shotguns, they hunted roebuck, roe deer and wild deer all over the mountains..."

The well-known song vividly pictures the hunting lifestyle of the Oroqen people. Since ancient times, they peopled the deep forests of the outer and inner Kinggan Ranges and the Heilongjiang Valley, known as "the huntsmen of the Khingan Range". Accompanied by animals, Oroqen people believe in the unity of heaven and man and that everything in the world has a spirit. Their religion is shamanism and their objects of worship range from the sun, the moon, the wind and the thunder to mountains and rivers. Shamans, as messengers between men and gods, are mostly female. They are regarded as wise prophets, carrying the hope of the Oroqen people for their daily lives and work. When suffering from bad weather or a serious disease, Oroqen people would turn to the shamans to end the disaster with their power.

"Even if you wander outside for one year, there is no need to worry as the welkin will protect you from the winds and rains." These words depict the bold lifestyle the Oroqen people once led. In 1953, dozens of tribes made up of over 100 Oroqen people in the Aihui County in Heilongjiang Province ended their original nomadic way of living—building houses with birch barks, wearing clothes made of pelts and feeding on animal meat—with the support of the government. They settled down at the bank of Cierbin River and leap-frogged several historical stages to a socialist society from a primitive communal society. That's the birth of the Xinsheng Village at the Autonomous Village for Oroqen People at the Aihui District, Heihe City. Through training and practice, Oroqen People could drive tractors as skillfully as they handled shotguns. They could grow crops as well as gather wild vegetables as before. A new chapter in their history thus began. That's why the village is called "Xinsheng" (meaning newborn).

Xinsheng Village is the seat of the township government and favorably situated. It is surrounded by mountains, dense forests and crystal clear water. The fertile land presents picturesque sceneries all year round: the azaleas blossom bright as fire in spring, the green sea of woods in summer, the crimson maple all over the mountains in autumn and the snow-wrapped world in winter. More than 60 oroqen families comprise the less than 200 remaining oroqen. Some Oroqen people have been assimilated by the Hans due to intermarriage. The long-standing nomadic lifestyle led to the birth of the unique living Shamanism culture while the rich animal and plant resources ensure the survival of the Oroqen culture in Xinsheng Village. It is known as "the first hunting village in Northern China".

Although the villagers are now leading a relatively modern life, they still wear the traditional clothes of the Oroqen people. Their houses are decorated with various handicrafts like pelts, knitting as well as artifacts made from birch barks and bones. Visitors can also watch the process of making handicrafts and make one themselves.

When the Oroqen people first moved downhill, they lived in primitive conditions. The wooden and earthen brick houses were covered by special grasses. Later these houses were changed into brick and tile houses with the roofs and ridges decorated in the same way as that of the traditional wooden tents. The houses are now furnished with cable TV, mobile phones and running water. The rich villagers even own cars. The storehouse is full of soybeans and the yard is filled with kidney beans piled up like hills.

In Xinsheng Village, visitors can taste the game and go canoeing in boats made of birch bark, drifting on the Huma River, or go horse-riding, play archery or go fishing by the riverside. In the evening, the Oroqen girls often sing and dance. Visitors can join them and forget the fatigue of the day.

Tourists can also visit the traditional dwellings of Oroqen people called "*xianrenzhu*" , which is similar to the tent of North American Indians. With pine or birch poles serving as the main supporting frames, it is enclosed with stitched birch barks while in winter it will be covered with the skins of wild animals. It is usually five or six *meters* in height and seven or eight *meters* in diameter. Some gaps are reserved on the top to release smoke and get light. In the center of the ground is a hearth for cooking, heating and illumination. Usually there is a warehouse made of birch bark near *xianrenzhu* where the food huntedis stored. In the evening, the elderly will sit around the bonfire and tell the kids fairy tales. Hunters will perform the lively "Black Bears Fight Dance" to convey their awe for the god of fire. They are covered with red cloths, which add a mysterious and primitive sense of the forest. These represent the god of the mountain respected by the Oroqen people. In the past, every time when hunters were about to go hunting for tigers, bears or other large beasts, they would make sacrifice to pray for harvest and a safe return.

The Oroqen people love forests and have a special veneration for the woods. As they are familiar with the mountainous roads and good at riding horses, they have become the guides for the teams for fire-fighting, forest investigation and geologic prospecting. There is also a team of riders and forest guards in Xinsheng Village who keep patrolling up the mountains and guarding the forests, combating poaching and illegal logging, even helping with chasing criminals and drug prohibition. It's a really tough job: the bites of mosquitoes, snakes and ants in spring and summer, the threats from roaring wind and chilly frost in autumn and winter and the dangers of ferocious animals like black bears and wild boars out of nowhere. With a melodious chant, a group of riders rush across the dense forest. The Oroqen people with a dark complexion, narrow eyes and high cheekbones are performing their duties, leaning forward on horseback and carrying their shotguns. These are the forest guards. Although the Oroqen people are now leading a modern lifestyle, their ethnic culture and heroic sentiments handed down from generation to generation will never fade away.

The Oroqen people have a lot of etiquette. When they meet at the hunting ground or on the way, the young will dismount from his horse immediately and stand by the road and mount up again until the senior has left. When guests come, the host will welcome them warmly and greet them with courtesy while the hostess makes a low bow with her hands on her forehead. Then the guests are invited into the house. The family shall treat the guests to their best food. The first dish served is milk tea while the staple food is animal meat. The Khingan Range is home to various wild animals like deer, roe deer, boars and bears. A variety of fish abound in the crisscrossed network of rivers. These serve as a sufficient source of necessities for the Oroqen people. It is the men's job to go hunting and fishing. They spear Brachymystax lenok, Hucho taimen and chum salmon with iron forks and boil them with wild leek and coast banksia. These specialties are quite delicious. The Oroqen women have marvelous skill in making fur and birch bark products. The birch bark is corrosion free and not prone to distortion. Birch bark peeled in May or June can be turned into barrels to contain water and milk, baskets to carry food, cigarette cases and even sewing kits. These objects are not only functional but exquisite. The birch bark can also be made into boats. This type of boat is light but firm. It can hold up to 200 to 250 *kilograms* but can be shouldered by only one person.

Over the long history of living in the forest, pelt serves as the main material for clothes. Pelts acquired from hunting in different seasons can be processed into garments, boots and hats, quilts or sleeping bags by Oroqen women depending on the respective quality of the material. To make full use of leather, Oroqen women turn the offcuts into beautiful pockets, sachets, belts and decorations for hunting knives. Meng Lanjie, an old lady living in Xinsheng Village, is the national intangible cultural heritage bearer of the Oroqen roe deer pelt production craft. The unique roe deer pelt keeps its original warmth while the continuity of cultural tradition reflects the wish of the Oroqen people.

The Gulunmuta Festival, which is unique to the Oroqen people, takes place on August sixth annually. Visitors can feel the hospitality of the Oroqen people on that day: the stirrup cup kindly offered, maidens presenting garlands and there is singing and dancing. It is customary of the Oroqen people to go hunting on the mountains after the first snowfall every year. Now, people drive the trunk up the mountain to carry the game back, which is more efficient and convenient.

The forests and rushing rivers of the Khingan Range witnessed the nomadic people thrive, migrate and integrate on this fertile land. They still live there, carrying on the ancient customs and the spiritual traditions of hunters. Yet some changes have taken place. The Oroqen people now have a wider vision, increased income and more fashionable lifestyle. After walking out of the forests over 60 years ago, the Oroqen people and their Xinsheng Village have become a specimen, displaying the evolutionary combination of traditional and modern civilization.

^村子边缘——鄂伦春人的建筑别具一格，将道路命名得非常浪漫

The edge of the village — Oroqen buildings are very special and the names of roads sound quite romantic

< 勤劳的中国农民是中华民族的典型代表，他们每一天都面对不同的农活，虽然辛苦，但却乐在其中

Hard-working farmers represent the typical character of diligent Chinese people. they have to do different hard work of farming in the field everyday but they find pleasure in it

^新生村地处偏远山区，地多人少，交通工具是必不可少的帮手，这里的鄂伦春人每家都有一台或者是几台规格不一的拖拉机

Xinsheng Village is located in a remote mountainous area. Transport is indispensable to such a place with a vast land and a small population. Here every Oroqen family has one or more tractors of different sizes

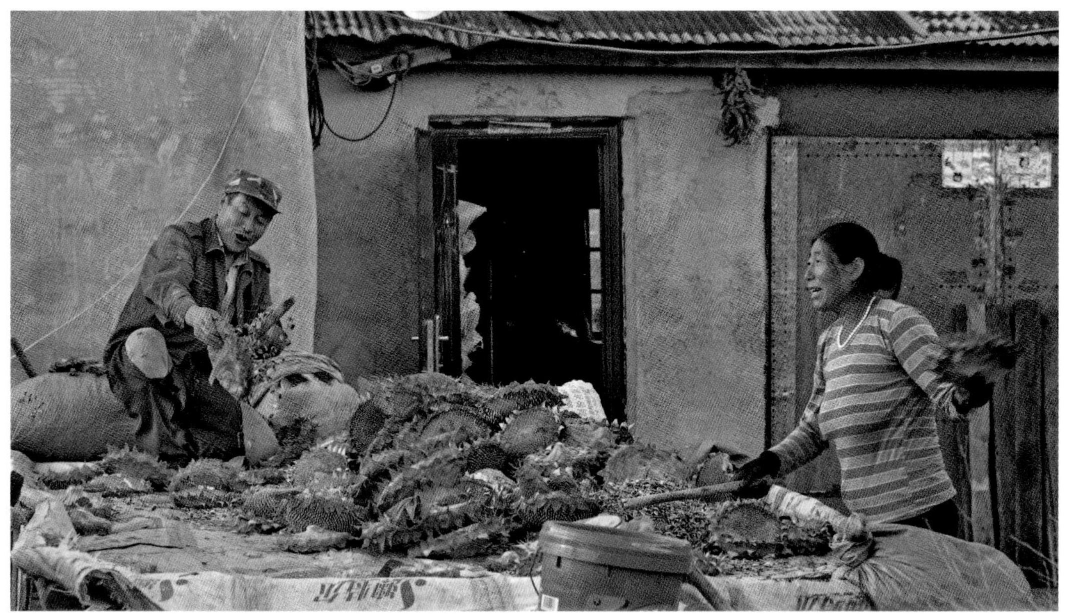

^喜获丰收的季节，村民在各家院里搭起了架子，敲打着葵花子，晾晒后，连吃带卖，每个人的脸上都露出了幸福的笑容

Each family has built a stand in the yard at the harvest time. People are beating the sunflowers for seeds. They can either enjoy the dried seeds as a snack or sell them for money. That's when a happy smile appears on the face of each person

03

松岭屯

调查报告原文 / 摄影
王彬

Reported / photograghed by
Wang Bin

> 松岭屯的房屋坐落在山区，房屋都是依山而建的

Located in a mountain area, houses in Songling Village are built based on topography

云山绕村翠梦深

清朝末年，中原战乱频繁，加上自然灾害，土匪横行，民不聊生。而关外则是地广人稀，物产丰富。是内地人民特别是山东一带的百姓把东北视作安身立命的希望。他们挈妇将雏、举家迁徙，辽东走廊浩荡的逃难人群延续上百年，这就是闯关东。闯过关东的人们像撒播种子一样在东北的黑土地上生发芽，形成了一片片村落。

吉林省临江市花山镇松岭屯就是这样形成的山东屯之一。沿着沟膛子，村落错落有致地绵延几千在这片曾经荒无人烟的山地上，数代村民凭借勤劳的双手开辟梯田、搭建茅屋，逐渐习惯了近千米的海拔和冬季的严寒，以完全农耕的方式实现了安居乐业的梦想。

松岭屯位于临江市花山国家森林公园，在通化至临江铁路最长的隧道——老岭隧道东侧出口处，为人所知，还得归功于艺术工作者。从 20 世纪 90 年代起，一些摄影家和画家跋山涉水来到这里采风考

它为原型的水墨丹青被媒体报道，从而吸引了游客纷至沓来。

由于地处深山，海拔较高，这里的春天比起平原来得晚一些，直到 5 月中旬花儿才大面积放。村民们家家户户房前屋后栽种着李子树、梨树、杏树等。花期一到，满山粉色、白色的花，似香雪海。冰雪融化成汩汩的清泉，田地里劳作的人也多了起来，整个松岭屯都充满了生机。于农作物的生长期比较短，农田都覆盖了地膜以促进作物发育。蜿蜒的地膜在李子花的映下闪闪发亮，更显妩媚动人，也成为这里的一道特殊风景。晚春，野百合含苞待放，似点点焰跳跃在绿野山坡、路旁、农家院子里。还有沁人心脾的野玫瑰和各种不知名的野花，能够闹整个夏天。

松岭屯最有特点的季节还是冬天。没有春天那漫山遍野的梨花、杏花像云彩萦绕在山坡，

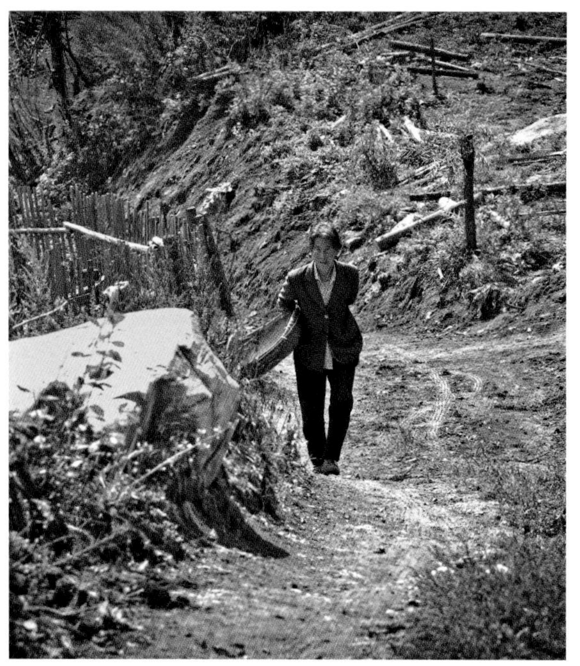

没有夏日山风送爽、水流潺潺以及云霞流香，没有深秋层林尽染一片金黄，95%以上的冰雪覆盖率过滤掉了地上的绝大部分色彩，只剩下黑白灰的团块和蜿蜒的线条，在镜头下恰似一幅水墨画，吸引了国内外摄影爱好者来此摄影，被誉为关东雪村，水墨松岭。

山里过年也别有一番热闹。腊月到正月，被树木和远山环抱的雪村张灯结彩，像在泼墨画中点缀着一点点艳红，格外耀眼。采购年货的牛爬犁在雪地上留下道道车辙。“莫笑农家腊酒浑，丰年留客足鸡豚”，在民风淳朴的村里，游客经常被热情地邀请到村民家里把酒言欢。作为山东人的后裔，村民的饮食还没有离开馒头、煎饼，说话仍是纯正的山东口音。这里的年菜以炖菜为主，再搭配几口东北的高粱酒，真是吃在嘴里，乐在心里。也有用长白山人参、鹿茸、雪蛤、松茸蘑等数十种山珍制成的佳肴，用来招待最尊贵的客人。

松岭虽然地势高寒，但土壤肥沃、物产丰富，犹如聚宝盆。村民们既掌握平原农民的传统农耕手艺，又跟山民学会了采集、渔猎。这里的农田很有特色，依山势而开，线条曲折但统一，光滑的地膜与粗糙的褐色土地形成强烈反差。间或有农舍散于其中，掩映着些树木，正像中国传统山水画经常描绘的山居图。

提到梯田，虽有中国云南的元阳梯田驰名中外，可吉林的松岭，勤劳智慧的农民随山势地形变化而开垦梯田不逊于元阳。这里的梯田虽然被山势所限，不像阳梯田那样气势开阔，但站在山头远眺，黄、白、绿相线条的蜿蜒曲折，加上远景中流动的山泉和浓淡不一密林，仿佛一幅神秘而悠远的抽象画。

除了满目风景，松岭屯还给其子民准备了各种山从春到秋，浆果、野菜、菌蘑等源源不断。最有名的要属榛粒大饱满，油分足。村民们经常在周日背着山货和自产农作物到城里去赶集：前一天坐火车到市里，花5元住在站前的小旅店，第二天再去集市把货物卖掉。尽卖不了多少钱，但换回些生活必需品就满心欢喜。

前些年春节一过，村里的青壮年就陆续外出打留下老人和少数孩子。田间院落散落着一丝落寞的味村里有所小学，红瓦白墙，校园周围长满荒草，偌大的园只有几个孩子在读书，其余的孩子都随父母外出打了。如果给村民拍一张合影，招呼过来的大半是60岁上的老人，偶尔有一两个缠着爷爷奶奶的幼童。

随着新农村建设进程的加快，外出打工的村民有流的趋势。人们开办起了农家乐，盖起了新房子，平整道路，出行也自如了。每年来这里旅游的人数是本地口的几十倍，且还在持续增加。曾经散落山间无人识小山村也面临着从未有过的挑战：青山绿水会不会被发商破坏？生活垃圾会不会掩埋掉各个角落里的野花快餐食品的流入，是不是会改变人们绿色健康的饮食惯？交流的增多会不会让纯朴的村民变得油滑？

站在山岗上，任风吹过，静谧的小山村让人的心格外平静。但愿这股清风也能够抚平乡村开发的浮躁气，让这里的安宁一直延续下去。

< 松岭屯的人

A local people in Songling Village

^ 松岭屯的房屋坐落在山区，
房屋都是依山而建的

Located in the mountain area, houses in Songling Village are built along the terriain

Songling Village

In the late Qing Dynasty, frequent wars in the Central Plains coupled with natural disasters and rampant banditry, took the people there through a time of hardship and difficult survival. Meanwhile, due to the fact that the vast area outside of Shanhaiguan Pass in northeast China remains sparsely populated and prolific, some residents in the plains, particularly those from Shandong Province, began considering this area a dream land to live a new life. They strove to flee from calamity by migrating entire families to the eastern and southern parts of Liaoning province, and here began the so-called "Brave Journey to Northeast China" that lasted over a hundred years. Since then, these migrant people have built villages in northeast China to settle down, like seeds sowed in the land of Black Soil[1], to take the root and sprout.

With a nickname of "Shandong Village", Songling Village is located in Huashan Town, Linjiang City, Jilin Province. Stretching several *kilometers* along the valley, houses in Songling Village are well spaced and arranged. After many generations of effort to reclaim wasted land into terraces and huts, the village has been developed from a desolate and uninhabited mountainous field to a livable land, and villagers have been gradually accustomed to the high altitude of nearly one *kilometer* and the freezing winter, realizing their dream of living a prosperous and contented life through farming.

Songling Village lies near the Huashan National Forest Park and the east exit of Laoling Tunnel, which is the longest tunnel along the railway from Tonghua City (Liaoning Province) to Linjiang City. It owns its current fame to artists. Starting in the 1990s, a number of photographers and painters made arduous journeys to this village to get sketches and images of its distinctive landscape. With their keen observation and strong sense of beauty, the artists created works based on the village's scenery which is as beautiful as Chinese water-and-ink paintings. These works, after being publicized through media, have attracted a large number of tourists.

Spring here in the high-altitude mountains comes later than in the plain, and flowers don't fully blossom until mid-May. Almost every household here plants plum trees, pear trees and apricot trees around their houses. When the flowe season comes, white and light-pink delicate petals fall over the land, just like sweet snow dancing with the wind, and the actual ice and snow melt into gurgling springs. Villagers als begin their work in the farmland, and the whole village is filled with warmth. Due to the relatively short growth period of crops, villagers adopt plastic mulching technology to ensure stable crop development and growth. Serpentine plastic mulches sparkle under the sun against plum flowers providing photographers with a unique view to present the scenery. Then comes the late spring when wild lilies are in bud. These buds are like little sparks covering the green field and the hills and decorating the village roads as well a the yards. Together with the refreshing scent of wild rose as well as the beauty of unnamable wild flowers, they make th scene enjoyable for the whole summer.

However, the most distinctive scenery in Songling Village always appears in winter. Unlike in the spring when flowers of pear and apricot blossom all over the hillside like rosy clouds, in the summer when breeze brings the villagers pleasant coolness and rivers and streams gurgle, and in the late autumn when the village is inflamed with autumnal gold en tints, Songling in the winter is covered by ice and snow f 95% of its land, since it sits in the cold Changbai Mountains Range. All colors in the village are filtered out, leaving only black, white and grey blocks and some sinuous lines. It is th distinct character that makes the village seem like, particularly in front of cameras, a Chinese traditional water-and-in painting, attracting both domestic and foreign photography enthusiasts. Therefore, Songling Village is also called "a typical snow village of northeast China and representative of ink-painting sceneries".

Villagers in Songling celebrate the Spring Festival in a special and lively way. When the first and twelfth lunar month come, surrounded by distant mountains and neighboring trees, the village is decorated by lanterns and colored hangings and banners, causing the black and white ink-picture to be adorned by several bright red figures, thus oking glamorous and attractive. The cattle-drawn sleighs, ansportation tools used by villagers to do special purchas- for the Spring Festival, leave ruts in the snow field. As Lu u, a prominent poet of China's Southern Song Dynasty , ıce wrote in a poem, "Don't sneer at the lees in the peas- ıts wine; in a good year they've chicken and pork to offer ıests", people are simple, honest and hospitable in the lage. Guests are often invited by villagers to their houses converse cheerfully over glasses of wine. As descendants people from Shandong Province, villagers still keep the ıbit of mainly eating steamed buns and Chinese pancakes, ıd speak with a Shandong accent. They prepare sumptu- ıs food and dishes for the traditional Chinese New Year, ost of which are stewed food in *kaoliang* spirit (a famous ıinese spirit in northeast China). Every bite is taken with e happy mood. Among all the foods, the most luxurious ıe, which not only is delicious but also can strengthen one's dy, is the feast made of dozens of precious ingredients, ch as ginseng from Changbai Mountains, pilose antlers, ıinese Forest Frogs and Tricholoma matsutake. This feast ll only be served to the most distinguished guests.

In spite of being located in an extremely cold area, ongling Village is super abundant in agricultural products the land is fertile, as if people are sitting on a pot of gold. llagers are both skilled in farming like traditional peasants the plains, and hunting and fishing which they learned from ountaineers. The farmland is quite distinctive, as the land ought under cultivation is based on topography, sinuous t unified. The smooth plastic mulch shows striking con- ast with the brown rough land. Farmhouses are scattered in os and threes, and together with the flowering fruit trees, ey form a picture displaying dwelling in the mountains ıich could be commonly found among traditional Chinese ndscape paintings.

When it comes to bench terraces, most people would ink of the Rice Terrace in Yuanyang (Yunnan province) as s famous both at home and abroad. However, the bench rrace in Songling, which was developed by industrious and se Songling farmers based on the topographic changes, is

^松岭屯的人

A Songling Villager

> 随手挂在门口的农具

Farm implements casually hang in the doorway

in fact not inferior to it. Limited to the topography, the terrace in Songling is not as vast and vigorous as the field in Yuanyang, but it demonstrates another picture. Overlooked from the top of the mountain, the terrace field alternates with three colors, namely yellow, white and green, winding naturally and smoothly, and looks mystically distant like an abstract painting when gurgling mountain springs as well as the combination of shades from groves join in.

1. Black Soil: Black Soil refers to the color of rich cultivated land in northeast China.

In addition to the eye-catching scenery everywhere, Songling village is also known for its abundant mountain products available from spring to autumn, such as berries, potherb, fruits, vegetables, mushrooms and dried foods. The plump-eared and oily hazelnuts are the best-known of all. On Sundays, villagers usually carry bags of mountain products and home-grown crops to go to town and sell them at the market. Departing for the town on the first day by train and spending five yuan on board at an inn near the railway station, the villagers will sell the products the next day at the market. Although they cannot earn a large fortune on it, villagers are still happy about exchanging the products for some necessities of life.

In previous years, young villagers would begin to leave for work soon after the Spring Festival, leaving only elder people and children at home; and even the courtyards seemed lonely and aloof from the world. There was a primary school in the village, with red roofs and white walls, and overgrown weeds and wild trees. Only a few children were studying in this spacious campus, as the rest had left with their parents and went to school in cities where their parents were working. If you'd like to take a photo of the villagers, most of the people who you'd capture would be over 60 years old, occasionally with one or two little children accompanying the grandparents.

In recent years, with the acceleration of new rural construction, more and more migrant workers choose to go back home to build new houses, develop farmhouse tourism, and mend the road for convenient transportation. Nowadays, the number of yearly tourists here is dozens of times that of the local residents, and is consistently increasing, and this small village which is located in the mountains and was known to nobody before has to face unprecedented challenges. Villagers began to worry about issues like what if the developers spoil the beautiful country scene by unbridled construction of villas, garbage burying wild flowers in every corner, the introduction of fast food changing people' green and healthy diet, and strengthened communication with the outside world adds some glibness to the original and simple Shandong accent.

Standing on the hill with the breeze coming, people could gain calmness in this little village. There is a hope that the breeze could also carry away the fickleness caused by rapid rural construction so that the peace and calmness here could continue and last forever.

^ 乡间崎岖的小路

The rugged and winding country lane

< 松岭屯独具特色的民居，成了这里的旅游标志

Distinctive folk houses in Songling Village have become the landmark buildings for tourists to visit

> 山坡上的人家

A household residing on the hillside

∨ 松岭屯的人

Local people in Songling Village

04

大庄许家社区

调查报告原文 / 摄影
聂艳

Reported / photograghed by
Nie Yan

> 大庄许家社区民居

Folk houses in Dazhuang xujia Village

明崇祯年间，从安徽迁徙而来的许姓家族在山东省威海市荣成市俚岛镇建立了大庄许家社区。过一代代居民的打造，大庄许家社区成为山东半岛干净整洁、独具古朴胶东风味的美丽一角。湛蓝的空舒展着白云，一边是蓝丝绒般的大海，一边是连绵起伏的青山，这样的美景吸引着一批又一批的游

走进大庄许家社区，映入眼帘的是一排排整齐漂亮的住宅楼，楼下停放着轿车或摩托车，整洁的境和连片绿地使之呈现出半城半乡的混搭风格。一路走到社区中心，始建于清乾隆三十八年（1773 年的许氏宗祠就坐落在这里。经历了 200 多年的风风雨雨，至今完好无损，成为后人追思祖先的精神依目前，大庄许家社区有 200 多户人家，大部分是许氏后裔。

“先祖德望在，后辈业绩高”，一副对联挂在宗祠门前，黑砖砌墙，海草苫顶，房脊两头翘，中间

大，古朴典雅。祠堂平时不对外开放，只有到年末岁初供社区里的老人们携子带孙前来祭拜祖。那时的宗祠灯火通明，进进出出的男人们表情严肃，女人们提前几天就在忙碌着准备上用的花饽饽。

宗祠周围环绕的一排排海草房是大庄许家社区的老居民区。它们建于不同年代，垒石为墙，草为顶，错落有致，静谧深远。大庄许家社区是威海市保存海草房最多的地方，居民介绍说，在屋顶的海草随着风雨侵袭慢慢变薄变少，这时，居民会将晒干的海草补苫在破损的地方。年又一年过去了，最底层的海草可能有几十年甚至上百年的历史。老人们自豪地说："住海草安静，晚上睡觉特香，下多大的雨也听不见，不像瓦房那样叮叮咚咚敲鼓似的响。"海草房里藏着渔家的记忆,有荣成人的柴米油盐,离家远行的荣成人也常常想起住海草房的日子。

石墙的硬朗，海草的柔软，配上一根烟囱，常让慕名而来的文人、画家充满灵感，称海草房是童话里的房子。20 世纪 60 年代著名画家吴冠中来威海写生，看到数量众多的海草房后，写下这样的句子：

“那松软的草质感，调和了坚硬的石头，又令房顶略具缓缓的弧线身段。有的人家将废渔网套在草顶上，大概是防风吧，仿佛妇女的发网，却也添几分俏丽。”

走出祠堂，穿行在小巷中，有进入迷宫之感，更有曲径通幽之意。古朴厚重的石墙之上，有的还残存着“抗战胜利万岁”这样的标语。成片成行的无花果树，像是无声却温柔的守护者，任孩子们肆意攀爬，给人们带来溢满香甜的欢乐。

像爱护海草房一样，荣成人极爱护环境。大庄许家社区街道干净利索，蜿蜒的沙石路面即使在大雨过后也不会泥泞。随着居民生活水平的不断改善，这里也盖起了水泥小楼房，和原有的草房比邻而居。浅褐、灰白的海草房被崭新的水泥小楼环抱着，饱经风霜的石头墙依旧散发着暗红的光泽，一半古朴深沉，一半时尚新颖。历史与现代并不矛盾，记忆与现实同样可以完美交融。走进一户居民的家中，不禁感叹：这才是我们记忆中的农家小院——窗户上贴着美丽的窗花，屋外高高地摞着玉米垛，灶台

^ 胶东花饽饽

Jiaodong *huabobo*

上坐着呼呼冒着热气的大铁锅……好客的主人有着海边人家的纯朴，他们的房间布置仍保持着过去的风格，玻璃相框里叠放的老照片、印着花纹的梳妆镜、斑驳的烛台、倚放在窗台的烟袋锅，无不显示家庭氛围的温馨。

午后时分，漫步至东侧的纹石滩，人们正在整理养殖海带的粗绳和浮标，他们边干活边聊家常，爽朗的笑声在湿润的海风中回荡，全无困顿之苦。岸边静静泊着几条渔船，它们虽不能和渔港里的千帆云集媲美，但同样能与大海搏击，承担渔民养家糊口的重任。

社区东侧的这片海，如同母亲般给予了大庄许家人滋养。海滩有一个美丽的名字，叫纹石滩，这里也是当地人引以为傲的“宝藏”所在。据说有人在纹石滩上捡到一枚黄色奇石，呈三角形，上面隐约看见一个红圈和 3 座山，名曰日照三神山，当地富户想以八亩耕地交换奇石，未果。

漫步纹石滩，白色的细沙托举着一层厚厚的鹅卵石，大者若拳头，中者若卵，小者若豆，五颜六色、光彩夺目。石质也各有不同，有黑铁石、将军红石、翡翠石、黄玉石等，白如洁玉，红似玛瑙，绿若翡翠，令人叹为观止。传说在远古时代，几个龙王争霸此地，斗得天昏地暗。战斗结束后，海滩上留下了片片龙鳞，后来龙鳞就变成布满沙滩、光怪陆离的纹石，纹石滩由此得名。

除了海草房、纹石滩，这里还有一件与胶东人日常生活息息相关的特产——花饽饽！

胶东花饽饽早在汉代就有文字记载，宋代以来用作祭祀摆供。经过千年传承和发展，如今依旧盛行于胶东农村。花饽饽在不同节日有不同的表现形式和意义。清明节燕子归来、六月初八龙王寿诞、七月七牛郎会织女等时节的花饽饽各不相同。从腊月到正月十五，从孩子出生到老人做寿，结婚、上梁、百岁，人们都用花饽饽来表达庆贺和对亲人的祝福。

如今，会蒸花饽饽的人已经非常少了，其中手艺精湛的大多在 60 岁以上。好在胶东花饽饽已经被列入山东省级非物质文化遗产，并确立了传承人。

花饽饽以面粉为原料，一个个普通面团经过巧妇的双手，既可以被捏塑成千姿百态的人物形象，也可以被做成活灵活现的动物、鲜艳美丽的花草树木。造型简单夸张、神态生动传神、用色大胆泼辣，花饽饽既有浓厚的乡土气息，又具备传统绘画的神韵。

还有一种普通的枣饽饽，这是勤劳的胶东女人们所擅长的，它也是人们日常的主食。尤其是过大年，在大红灯笼的映照下，听着脆生生的鞭炮声，吃上一口白白胖胖的大枣饽饽，年味就来了！最大的枣饽饽，一口锅只蒸一个，有好几斤重，俗称团圆饽饽，讲究家里有几口人就在上面放几个枣，而且吃的时候不能切开，要每人掰下必须带个大枣的一块。最小的饽饽俗称莲子花，它是主妇们最常做的，没有复杂的工序，把面团塞进木质模具中按实，扣出来的就是一个个带着图案的小莲子花了。无论大、小饽饽，一定要在掀锅时看到每一个饽饽都被蒸裂了口，主妇们才会开心，这就意味着饽饽“笑了”，来年就会笑口常开、吉祥如意。

^孩子们在玩耍

Children are playing

Dazhuangxujia Village

During the reign of Emperor Chongzhen of the Ming Dynasty, Xu Family, which originated in Anhui Province, built Dazhuangxujia Village in Lidao County, Rongcheng City, Weihai City, Shandong Province. Years of diligent work have built this beautiful, clean and neat fishing village in its simple style with unique characteristics of the Shandong Peninsula. The village lies under the blue sky and white clouds, with the blue velvet sea flowing on one side and green mountains tolling on the other. It attracts waves of tourists.

Coming into Dazhuangxujia Village, one would see lines of beautiful residential buildings with cars and motorbikes parked in the open garage. The village shows a mixed style of urban and rural life with its modern buildings and farms. Walking all the way to the village center, one would see the ancestral shrine of Xu Family, built in 1773 during the reign of Emperor Qianlong of the Qing Dynasty. The shrine still remains in excellent condition after 200 years . Local people visit the shrine to remember their ancestors. At present Dazhuangxujia Village has 200 households, most of whom are the descendants of the Xu Family.

The shrine is a simple classic antique building. By the two sides of the gate hang two couplets, "Our ancestors are well respected; our future generations are highly accomplished." It uses black bricks for its walls and seaweed for the roof. The ridge rises higher at its two ends and sinks in the middle, giving itself a look of a disserted Northern ropean church in the wild. The shrine is not open to the blic except the beginning and end of the year. Old people Dazhuangxujia Village would bring their children and grand ildren here to pay tribute to their ancestors. At that time, e place is brightly lit. Men all wear a solemn face and wom- spend days to prepare *huabobo*, a famous local cuisine ade of flour, for the tribute.

The old resident block of Dazhuangxujia Village is rmed with lines of seaweed houses around the shrine. zhuangxujia village keeps the largest amount of seaweed uses in Weihai City. These houses were built in different es, using stones as walls, seaweed as rooftops. They lie in orderly fashion, all peacefully. A local villager tells us they uld not remove the seaweeds from rooftops, but as the nd blows and rain falls, there would be less and less sea- eeds. Then, villager would use dried seaweed to amend and ver any missing parts. Year by year, the seaweeds at the ttom might be decades old or even hundreds of years old. oking at the rooftops, one could feel the mottled sense history. Old people in the village say proudly: "you could eep in the seaweed house safely and soundly, because it is ry quiet within the house. No matter how heavy the rain is, e seaweed house would never make any noise like a tile- ofed house does." Local people's memory is deeply rooted the seaweed houses. Anyone who is far away from home uld often think of their times in the houses.

The solid stonewalls, the soft seaweed rooftops, gether with the chimney inspired the visiting writers and inters. They call it "the house of fairy tales". The fluffy eeds not only soften the hard stones, but make the roof- os more beautiful. Some families even wrap unused fishing ts over the top, perhaps as windproof, which is a bit like a male hair net. "It gives the houses a feminine touch" wrote Wu Guanzhong, a famous painter who visited here in the 60s after viewing the seaweed houses.

Walking out of the shrine and through the alleys, one ght get a sense of entering a maze or secluded paradise. u would see solid stonewalls, some of which still carry e slogan "Long lives the victory of the War of Resistance ainst Japan." The alleys are lined with fig trees, which and as kids' guardians in silence. Children can climb freely to the trees. The trees bring a nice fragrance and lots fun. Local people take care of their environment in the me way they care about their own houses. The trees in zhuangxujia are very clean, with no trace of plastic bags ating around. The winding gravel roads would not be cov- ed with mud even after heavy rains. Under the influence of urbanization, more buildings made of cement go up, stand- ing together with the old seaweed houses. Cement buildings surround seaweed houses, in light brown or grey. Their weather-beaten stonewalls still shine a dark red radiance. The village embraces the profound influence of history, as well as new, and novel fashionable ideas. Here, history does not contradict the modern trend and memory blends perfect- ly with the reality.

Visiting one of the local houses, we could not help being amazed. This is what we would expect of a small yard in the countryside. The window frames are decorated with beautiful paper-cuts; corncribs stand tall in the yard; big iron pots are boiling on the stove... The host treats us with great hospitality. The interior decoration shows the fashion char- acteristics of the past, with old photos stuck in the frame, a dressing mirror with printed patterns, rusty candlesticks, smoking pipes by the window stands, all of which record the sweet memories of this family.

In the afternoon, you could take a walk on the Wenshi Beach on the east of the village. Men and women are arrang- ing the ropes and floats used to grow kelp. The beach is filled with their chat and laughter. They really enjoy their lives. A couple of rusty old fishing boats lie on the beach. The boats are a bit rough compared to big ships, but they are important tools for local families to make their living.

The sea to the east of the village provides for people in Dazhuangxujia Village like a mother. The beach has a beautiful name, called Wenshi Beach. Local people are proud of this beach for it holds a "fortune". It is recorded that, someone picked up an amazing stone on Wenshi Beach. It is yellow and is in a triangular shape with a vague shape of a red circle and three mountains, namely "three holy moun- tains under the sun". A rich local man wanted to use eight acres of land in exchange for this stone but failed.

Take a walk on Wenshi Beach. You would see layers of pebbles lying on the white sands, with the big ones the size of a fist, medium ones the size of an egg and small ones the size of a bean. The pebbles are full of colors. They are made of different stones, such as black stone, red stones, emerald stones and yellow jades stone. The white pebbles look like jade, red ones like agate, green ones like emerald. Legend has it that during ancient times, one of the battles between dragon kings took place on this beach. After the battle, a couple of scales of the dragon kings fell onto the beach, which turned into spectacular Wenshi pebbles, thus comes the name of Wenshi Beach.

Besides the seaweed houses, Wenshi Beach, Dazhuangxujia Village is also well known for its special cuisine—"*huabobo*".

The earliest record of *huabobo* dates back to Han Dynasty. During the Ming Dynasty, this cuisine was used during the tribute ceremony. After over a thousand years of development, *huabobo* is very popular in Shandong villages. It could be used in all kinds of traditional festivals and contains different meanings. People make different shapes of *huabobo* on different occasions. For example, for tomb-sweeping day, people celebrate the returning of swallows; on the eighth of June in Chinese lunar calendar, people celebrate the birthday of the dragon king; on the seventh of July in Chinese lunar calendar, people celebrate the reunion of the Cowherd and the Girl Weaver... People make *huabobo* to express their wishes during Chinese New Year, to celebrate the birth of a child, birthday of the elderly, wedding, building of a new house and 100 years' birthday.

Now, only a few women could master the skills to make *huabobo*. The ones who are most talented are in their 60s. Fortunately, Shandong *huabobo* has been listed as an intangible cultural relic in Shandong Province. The successors of this skill have been selected.

Huabobo uses flour as ingredients. The dough transforms into human figures in various poses, vivid animal figures and beautiful trees and flowers through women's delicate hands. These figures are in simple but exaggerated shapes, with lively expressions and in bold colors. They show strong local tastes, as well as the spirit of traditional Chinese painting. A commonly seen form of *huabobo* is *zhengzaobobo*, a steamed bun with dried jujube fruit. It is the main food for local people. Almost every diligent woman in Shandong is good at making *zhengzaobobo*. Imagine it is the New Year, the house is decorated with red lanterns; the air is filled with the happy sound of firecrackers. One bite of the fluffy *zhengzaobobo*, you would truly feel the atmosphere of the New Year. The biggest *zhengzaobobo* is around several *kilos*. You would need a big pot to steam it. It is called *tuanyuanbobo*, meaning the *bobo* for family reunion. The amount of dried jujube fruit you use has to be the same of the amount of the family members. And you should not use knives to cut it. Every family member would break a piece with one dried jujube fruit. The smaller *bobo* is called *lianzihua*, meaning the lotus flowers. Housewives cook them all the time. It is easy to cook. You put the dough inside a wood mold and apply some pressure. Then, turn over the mold; you would have *lianzihua* with beautiful patterns on top. Once the *huabobo*, no matter big or small, is steamed, make sure it cracks. Housewives would be delighted to see a cracked *huabobo*, because it means the *huabobo* smiles, symbolizing a happy life in the coming year.

^ 苫海草房

Seaweed houses

∧∨苫海草房

Seaweed houses

< 老人与家园

An elderly woman
and her homeland

> 大庄许家祠堂

The ancestral shrine of Xu Family

大莊許家祠
先祖德望在

∨ > 胶东大花饽饽

Huabobo in the eastern area of Shandong Province

05

东烟墩社区

调查报告原文 / 摄影
聂艳

Reported / photograghed by
Nie Yan

> 东烟墩社区不大，其间只有这一条主街道，小路则多为砂石路面，弯曲而狭窄

In this small village of Dongyandun, there is a main road through the houses; others are mostly narrow, winding gravel lanes

山东省威海市荣成市俚岛镇东烟墩社区和大庄许家社区同样位于胶东半岛最东端，傍黄海之滨，依隐隐青山，同样的半城半乡，相似的民风，又各具特色。

东烟墩社区于明万历年间建村，据《荣成市志》和当地村碑记载，起先因邻近琵琶寨，故以寨为村名。琵琶寨是军寨，相当于现代的兵营，是明朝边防卫所屯守之处。十里一墩、八里一寨，琵琶寨是拥有千余千米海岸线的明朝威海卫边防的一部分，也是抗倭最前线。除了琵琶寨外，东烟墩社区的西侧还有一座烟墩山，这也是重要的军事设施，相当于报警的烽火台。因地处烟墩山东麓，琵琶寨后改名为东烟墩社区。据社区里老人回忆，琵琶寨直到 20 世纪 60 年代还有遗迹可寻，还存有呈正方形、长宽各约 200 米的土城墙，遗憾的是，平整土地之后，遗迹也消失了。

东烟墩社区与大庄许家社区相距仅 2.5 千米，社区中整齐漂亮的住宅楼与传统古朴的海草房相映

趣。社区现有海草房近百间，占到全社区房屋数的一半。主街两边的墙体被粉刷一新，知名画家绘制的大幅迎宾文化墙洋溢着居民对远方游客的热情。

威海市尚有9.5万余间海草房，分布于荣成市俚岛镇等21个乡镇的300多个渔村。这是代以来，渔民、盐民、屯田军户留给后人的财富，有些村落至今保存着近二三百年历史的海房。《荣成文化通览》一书记载，海草房的整个建造过程需有石匠、苫匠、瓦匠、木匠4个种的密切配合，共70多道工序，且全部为手工操作。

碧海蓝天，灰白色的海草房房顶在阳光的照耀下呈现出沉稳的银色，配上黄泥塑成的马式屋脊，愈显古朴稳重。为防大风和麻雀，有的屋顶上还罩着陈旧的渔网，给海草房增添渔风情。漫步在窄小的街巷，有时还能看到大门旁的墙壁上凸出的拴马石，岁月的打磨让拴马

^这是海草房建筑中典型的三合院，海草房屋顶保存完好，墙体结实

This is a *sanheyuan* , a typical seaweed courtyard houses, with its roof and solid walls well preserved

石的绳洞也变得光滑。这通常是胶东富裕人家的标志，过去只有大户人家才养得起大牲畜。后来耕田种地机械化了，一些较新的海草房的墙体上已经没有拴马石了，不过有些讲究的人家还会在院墙石块表面雕刻元宝纹等吉祥图案。

走遍山东，听到人们说得最多的一句话就是“你可真有福”。走进村庄见到最多的也是“福”临门。一个“福”字，代表的是所有人的盼头。一些讲究的人家会在院门里的影壁和外墙上刻画“福”字花纹，房门上张贴的镏金“福”字更不可少。在人家的小院门口信步游走，随时能感受到祝福和喜庆的气息。

如今沿海渔村村民生活富足，已经没有为衣食烦忧的人家了。很多海草房被砖瓦房、小洋楼替代，孩子们一个个成家立业，一对对搬离祖屋，剩下的就只有老人们。老人大多是不愿搬进新房的，他们舍不得老房子，舍不得旧家具，舍不得进进出出大半辈子的小院，更舍不得乡里乡亲、门前屋后的相互照应，简单而纯粹的情分。

在日新月异的海滨城市边缘，泛着咸味的海风轻轻吹拂着这些古老的民居，把脊背吹得高耸，把石墙吹出青苔，把海草吹出沟壑。

虽然年轻人大多住上了楼房，但他们不会远离家乡。毕竟靠海吃海，很多年轻力壮的渔民还是守着家乡继续生活，而他们的孩子也经常在居住的古宅里嬉闹，在绿树红花掩映的小巷中撒欢儿。看着衣着光鲜的孩子们或骑着城里买的小自行车或滑着时兴的滑板车穿梭在老街，老人们的皱纹都笑成了花。而对于孩子们来说，待他们成年离乡以后，在城市的玻璃幕墙里怀想海滨渔村的童年，也将是心底永远的乡愁吧。

胶东地区的渔村至今还是“男主外女主内”的生活方式，男人是支撑一家人生计的主要劳力，女人婚后大多不外出工作了，专心在家相夫教子，一日三餐照顾着老少几代人。这里的人们，大多肤色较深，体形也较粗壮，不管是小媳妇还是老奶奶，都喜欢穿着带有大花且色彩艳丽的服装。胶东妇女性格爽朗，声音分贝较高，勤俭持家且吃苦耐劳，无论大家小户，门前院内只要有空地都不会任它荒着，连边边角角处都栽满了花草、藤蔓和蔬菜，房前屋后处处生机盎然。

在安静的老屋间穿行，街巷并不算宽敞，汽车开不进来，居民们走亲访友习惯步行。时不时见到人们坐在院门口拉家常或者晾衣、择菜。若是跟他们打个招呼，主人就会热情地邀请你坐下来歇歇，闲话家常。

虽然居民们都很好客也很健谈，但要想把镜头对准他们还是有困难的。一拿起相机，大嫂们不是捂着脸就是赶紧躲到一边去，嘴里还喊着：“可别拍俺，满脸褶子不好看。”经过风吹日晒的脸颊上似乎泛起了害羞的红晕。不是她们不配合，而是她们真的质朴，觉得自己不上相，不会给客人的照片增色。还是上年纪的老人更平和从容，看到镜头既不会拒绝也不会躲避。一位拄着拐杖的大爷今年已经 93 岁高龄，耳聪目明，只是腿脚不太利落。看到相机屏幕上的照片，大爷缓缓地点点头，夸奖拍得不错。虽然老人家未必能看清屏幕上的人影，更多是出于对晚辈的宽慰和对游客的礼貌，但老人的礼仪和体贴更让人感动。

与海相邻的村子总是透着一股淳朴气息。这里的斑驳渔船、僻静小巷和家家户户门前晾晒的海货和粮食，见证着渔家人依靠大海繁衍生息的安宁富足……

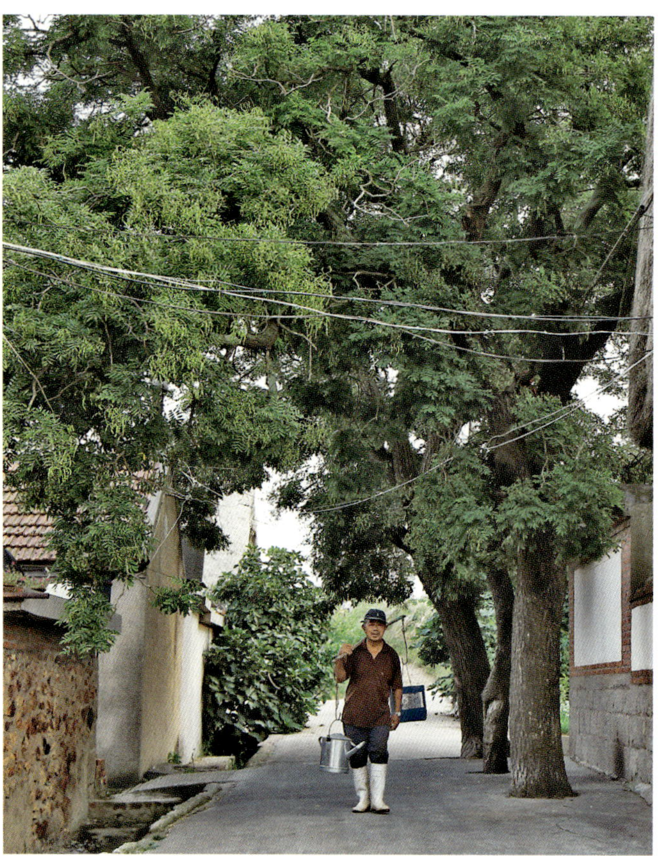

^老人刚从自家的地里浇水、施肥回来，他说，家里的地不多，干活只当锻炼身体了

This elderly person is back from the farm field after watering the crops. He said there was not much work to do and taking care of the land is exercise for him

Dongyandun Village

There are dozens of tourist attractions in Rongcheng of Weihai City, the easternmost of Shandong Peninsula. One of them is Dongyandu Village, which, along with Dazhuangxujia Village, belongs to Lidao Town which is located at the east end of Jiaodong Peninsula. Against the fair outline of mountains, those villages sit by the sic of the Yellow Sea. Both of them are part town an part village, sharing lots of customs, yet they are unique in their own way.

According to Roncheng City Catalog, durin the Wanli Period of the Ming Dynasty, the village was first named after Pipa Stockade Village because of their close location. An army stockade is similar to a military camp nowadays, and back in the Ming Dynasty it was the place where frontier defens armies were stationed. There was a mound every five *kilometers* , and a stockade village every four *kilometers*, forming the Weihaiwei defense station and t frontier against Japanese pirates. Another Yandun hill, standing at the west of Dongyandun Village, was another important military defense facility, functionin like a beacon tower for alerting. The old generation in the village said Pipa Villa existed until the 1960s. There was evidence such as square mud walls, with length and height at 200 *meters* or so. Later the relics vanished due to projects land repair and maintenance.

Dongyandun Village is only 2.5 *kilometers* away from Dazhuang Xujia Village. In this fishing village, there are traditional and unsophisticated seawee houses as well as beautiful countryside villas. Currently, almost 100 householc live in seaweed houses, accounting for half the families in the village. Walls by the main road were repainted. Famous painters and calligraphers were invited add their works on the walls to welcome tourists from afar, the villagers' way of showing hospitality.

In Weihai City, there are more than 9,500 seaweed houses, scattering ove 300 fishing villages of 21 towns and villages like Lidao. They are the fortune le by generations of fishermen, salt producers, stationed armies and farmers. Traditional seaweed houses with a history of up to 200 to 300 years can still be se in some of the villages. According to Rongcheng Culture Review, it requires close cooperation between stonemasons, thatchers, bricklayers and carpenters to complete over 70 manual steps to build a seaweed house.

Against blue sky and sea, the silver grey roof of the cottages, plus the saddle-like mud ridge, presents a sense of austere grace and calm demeanor. Some houses are covered by old fishing nets on their roofs to guard the thatched cover from strong winds and sparrows, giving it a more fishing house-style like feel. Down the narrow lane, hitching stakes for horses can be found on the walls by the doorway occasionally, and it becomes round and smooth after years of natural polishing. That is the symbol of rich families since in Jiaodong only big families could afford to keep large animals in the past. When agricultural activities started to depend on machines, people stopped building stakes on the walls of the relatively newer seaweed houses, yet the households who are meticulous about architecture would specifically carve some auspicious patterns like shoe-shaped gold ingots on the stone of the walls. These patterns may seem raw and crude, but they never lack the beauty on their own merits.

Travelling around Shangdong province, the most frequently heard phrase is "You are lucky". In the village, what's most common is the Chinese character "Fu" on the door, which displays people's hopes and prayers. Besides, some families with good taste in architecture have the screen wall and outer walling carved with patterns of the Fu character. You can feel the blessing and festivity passing by doors like these.

Nowadays, people in coastal villages have enough to eat and wear and some are living well-off lives. Seaweed houses are gradually replaced by tiles and bricks or countryside villas. Children have grown up, started their own families and left the elder at the ancestral homes. Most of the elderly are reluctant to move out of the old house, because they are "reluctant to leave. Certainly, years of company makes them emotionally connected, and they would be loath to part with the old house, the worn furniture and the courtyard they've been around for most of their lifetime, let alone the friendly and helpful neighbors.

As located by the rim of the ever changing coastal cities, the salty breeze gently stroked those old houses, turning the ridges higher and the thatch thinner, and let lichen grow on the stone walls.

Although most of the young generation has moved into buildings, they are not far away from home. A Chinese saying goes that those living near the water live off the water. Many young fishermen choose to stay at their hometown. The grandchildren can often go and visit their grandparents. They can still play and enjoy themselves on the paths covered by trees and decorated by flowers. For the old people, they cannot be any happier watching their grandchildren riding the small bicycles bought in town and playing skateboards on the old lanes. When these children grow up and move out, memories of their childhood in such a fishing village would always be cherished in the bottom of the heart.

In those old fishing villages of Jiaodong, people still honor the tradition of man being the breadwinner and woman the homemaker. Therefore, men are responsible for the livelihood of the whole family, while women are the housewives, taking care of the old and the children and being supportive of the husband. Living by the sea, men and women often get tanned skin and look quite strong. Jiaodong Women, no matter young or old, prefer colorful clothing with big flower patterns. They are straightforward and have very loud and bright voices. Being hard-working housekeepers, they never get lazy and let any of the land around their houses uncultivated. As they love beautiful things and life so much, flowers, vines and fresh vegetables are everywhere to be seen in the village.

To visit the old houses on the narrow lane, cars cannot make it. Villagers get used to walking to their neighbors. At times, you may see a housewife sitting by the doorway, chatting with old people while airing wet clothes or trimming vegetables. By saying hello you will definitely be invited by the hospitable host for a cup of tea and a casual chitchat.

This hospitality and easy-going demeanor, however, can hardly apply to the camera. Once the camera was on, the housewives either hide their faces or walked away, shouting "No, no, I am not good looking." Soon, a flush of rosy shyness came out on their weathered faces. Their reluctancy and refusal to take photos is not because they don't want to cooperate with us. Actually, in their simple and honest nature, they worry that they may deface the photos as they thought themselves not photogenic at all. In contrast, old people seem more clam in front of the camera, no turning people down or hiding. An elderly man walks slowly towards the camera on crutches. He is 93 years old but can still hear and see. Looking at the pictures taken on the camera screen, he nods his head slowly and said it was good. Though his words are more of encouragement and friendliness to the young visitor than his real feedback for the exact small figures on the photo, his courtesy and politeness are really touching and making people comfortable.

Villages adjacent to the sea always assumed a sense of simplicity and purity. The scattered fishing vessels, quiet lanes, sea products and grain in front of the households are the witnesses of the peaceful and affluent life of the fishing families···

∨一副手写的朴实的贺寿对联，一地刚刚燃放过的喜庆炮仗，这里是一户平凡而和睦的人家

A simple hand written couplet expressing birthday wishes on the wall and the shreds of firecrackers on the floor offer a glimpse of an ordinary but happy family

^ 俯瞰东烟墩社区，依山傍水，风景秀丽

Looking down onto the Dongyandun neighborhood, it is a beautiful village surrounded by lovely hills and the blue sea

> 老人每天的工作就是在家照看孙子

The elderly woman told the photographer happily that looking after her grandson at home is her daily routine

∨用大锅蒸花饽饽时必须用柳篾做的盖子，老人说他闲来无事，想试着给老伴做个新的

To make big rice bread, it requires the steamer cover made of willow splints. The elderly man said he wanted to make a new one for his wife in his abundant leisure time

^ 在这里，“福”字随处可见

In this village, the Chinese character “Fu” is everywhere

> 秋收季节，家家户户都忙碌起来

During the season of harvest, every households gets busy

06

东楮岛村

调查报告原文 / 摄影
毕延长

Reported / photograghed by
Bi Yanchang

> 伏天休渔，一艘艘的渔船静静地躺在宁静的港湾

In the dog days of summer, fishing boats are moored alongside the quiet harbour

摊开中国地图，山东半岛像是一只白天鹅探头伸进湛蓝的渤海湾。在“天鹅”的长喙与海水相接地方，山东大陆架最东端，有一个向阳避风的长条形半岛——楮岛，隶属荣成市石岛管区。明朝以附近的渔民在出海间隙常常在这里休息，岛周围栽满楮树，楮岛由此得名。后来陆续有居民来岛上定形成了渔村——东楮岛村。它是胶东地区保留最完好的古村之一，被誉为生态民居的活标本，被列入一批国家级传统村落保护名录。

这是一座呈荷花状展开的村子，地势东高西低。北、东、南三面环海，只有村西的一条路与大陆相陆地面积约 80 万平方米，可耕种土地约 26 万平方米，海岸线约长 10 千米，有近 200 户居民。

几百年来，东楮岛村村民们在这块海天相接的小岛上过着平淡从容的农耕渔猎生活，妈祖是这的保护神。传说，明万历年间，几艘正在海上行驶的渔船遇到风暴，眼看渔船就要被巨浪掀翻。船上

机灵的后生（方言：青年男子）想起老人曾经讲过的妈祖娘娘，遂带众人跪于船头，齐声高“妈祖娘娘保佑，妈祖娘娘保佑”。顿时，风浪平息，从压顶的乌云中闪出一道祥光，阳光重普照大地。渔船不仅没翻，反而满载归来。为了感念妈祖娘娘的恩德，众人在岸边建起一座娘庙。从此，东楮岛村风调雨顺，年年丰收。

岁月的积淀给村人留下一层层记忆，也让他们对脚下的土地充满感情。为了不忘根，他们集了木帆船、石磨、犁、耧等近百件先民使用过的生产生活用具，在村子西南角一座古朴的落里建起一间东楮岛村乡村记忆馆。走进展馆，那些裹挟着海风的故事迎面而来，就像打开坛尘封的老酒。或许因为处于闭塞之地，这里的村民格外重视文化教育，希望子孙能够走出岛，在更为宽广的大地上闯荡四方。早在 1936 年，村人就用卖扇贝的钱建起东楮岛村育英

学，这成为当时荣成境内最好的村办学校。现在的乡记忆馆就建在当年育英小学的校址上。

漫步东楮岛，近处一排排淡褐色的海草房错落有致、朴厚重。轻柔的海风送来淡淡的鱼腥味和海藻的味道。座北方渔村，既有海洋文化的粗犷，又有农耕文化的适，随着寒暑气候的变化，显现出不同的风采。有时和宁静，和风细浪；有时激昂慷慨，惊涛拍岸。它是摄家的福地，画家的世外桃源。

这里最奇异的景色就是那些顶着毛茸茸"帽子"的草房了。它们细致密实，像做工上好的毛绒外套抵御北方的朔风，沉淀着浓郁的地域文化，承载着淳朴的俗风情，是难得的原生态艺术品。全村现有海草房约0栋，其中百年以上历史的有80多栋。村子被国家建部、国家文物局命名为中国历史文化名村，被山东省命为乡村记忆示范村。中央电视台《远方的家——沿海行》目也曾为这里做过专题报道。

海草房多为方形院落，一进三合院或四合院。大门东南向，进门后一般迎面竖着一座影壁。正房三四间，西两厢房。围墙用大石块砌成，线条粗犷，随方就圆，样灵活，寓朴于美；房顶为木质檩、梁和椽子，内墙用板隔断。

海草房的房顶高高耸起，形似"将军帽"，让雨水不积存。苫盖屋顶所用的海草学名为大叶海苔草，是附海岸独有的野生藻类。它含大量盐卤、胶质，晒干后防蛀、防霉烂且不易燃烧。用其苫成的屋顶使用百年还坏不漏，冬暖夏凉，居住舒适。

古老的村落里忽然有了新生机，风力发电的风车成一道亮丽的风景线

w vitality is brought to this village – the windmill has come a beautiful scene

海草房的苫盖极具章法，是一门代代传承的手艺。建造时，一层麦秸加一层海草，层层叠压，拢成浑厚优美的曲线。屋顶再用瓦片或水泥压脊，有助于抗住大风。烟囱透草而出，每到傍晚，袅袅炊烟缓慢升腾，形成薄薄的雾岚，从村子向近海弥散，在空荡荡的渔船上方氤氲而去。一股人烟气息四散开来，温暖、温情。

在历经百年风雨侵蚀后，有些海草房的屋脊已经塌陷，海草变得斑驳松散，有些房子的外墙抹上了水泥，屋顶换成了砖瓦，历史的印记在消失。走在斑驳的青石板小巷，仿佛行进在岁月的长廊。一排排草房默然矗立，看着来来往往的行人。青石墙边的拴马石、山墙上的黑板报和标语是回忆那些逝去岁月的线索，提醒你那些或喧闹或平静的日子。

尽管传统的渔业和农耕生活方式日渐式微，但聪明的村民已经意识到祖先的遗产正是村子最大的财富。他们修缮房屋、整旧如新、拓宽道路、改善卫生，将村子进行保护性开发，大力发展民俗旅游业，将村子打造成海洋文化风情村。还建起了海草房国际艺术交流中心、海草房博物馆、观海长廊和游客服务中心。除了每年的胶东传统文化盛会——谷雨祭海节吸引大批游客之外，不少游客千里迢迢赶来，只为住一天海草房、吃一天渔家饭、睡一天农家炕、当一天渔家人，欣赏岛、湾、礁、石完美环绕的景观，感受质朴旷达的渔家气息。

走进一进三合院的院落，穿过长长的石板走廊来到北屋，陈年的木板隔墙已经发黑。左侧是土坯垒砌的锅灶，周围堆满柴火。传统的铁锅已经使用了几十年，锅盖是木质的。除了电灯和一台不大的电视机，见不到一点现代生活的气息。房东大爷已经80多岁，他说："祖上留下这海草房已有几百年了，我出生在这里，对它有感情，一辈子离不开它了。"一席话，道出了老人对乡土乡情的眷恋，道出了老一辈人对地域文化的坚守。他们，才是东楮岛村的灵魂。

Dongchudao Village

On the map of China, Shandong Peninsula reaching in Bohai Bay looks like a swan flying up towards the blue sky. At the place where the beak of the swan joins the sky – the east end of Shandong continental shelf – lies a strip-shape peninsula, a suntrap called Isle Chu, which is under the jurisdiction of Rongcheng City, Shandong Province. Ever sinc the Ming Dynasty it was a place where nearby fishermen regularly came to take a rest during the intervals of fishing. People planted trees called *Chu* (paper mulberry) all aroun it and that is how it is named. Gradually, people inhabited the isle and it became a fishing village named Dongchudac

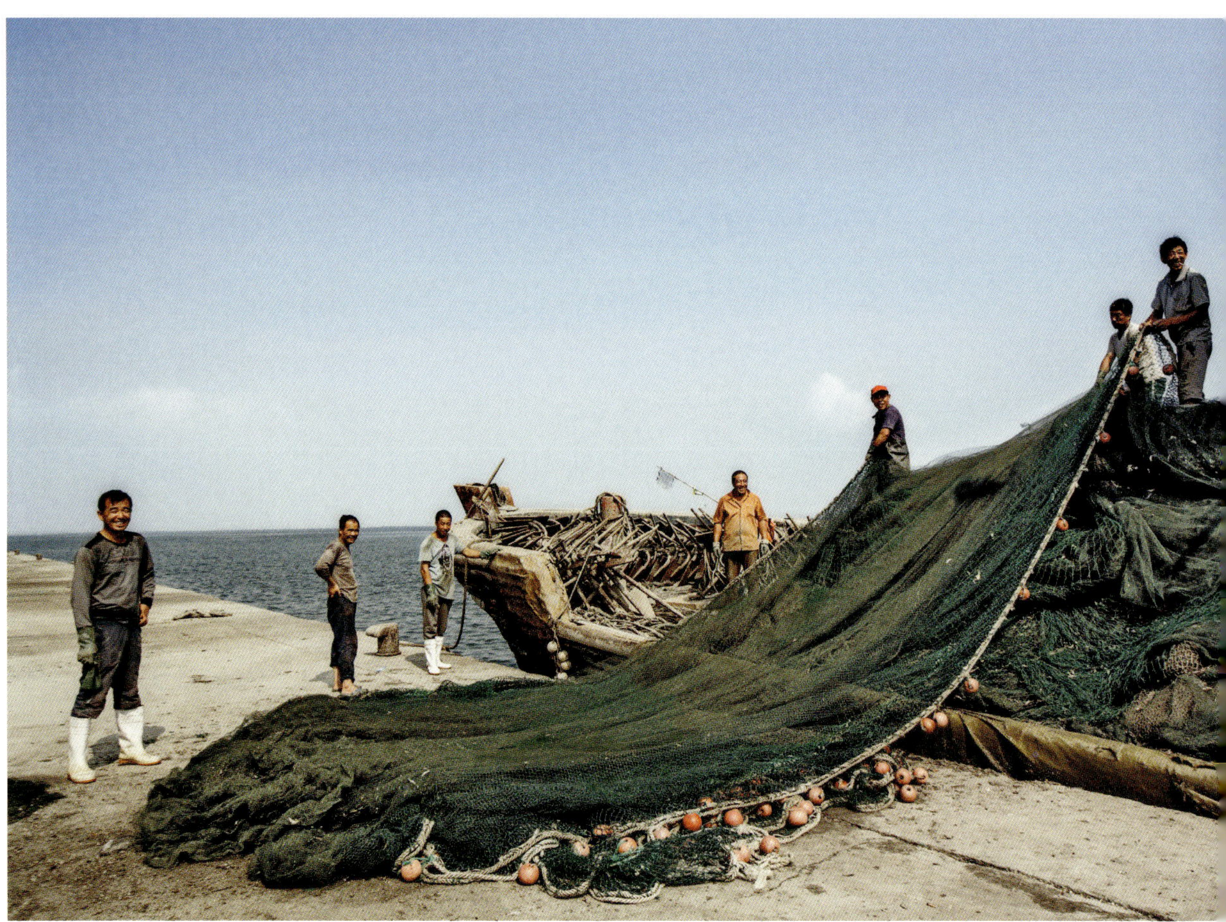

^唱着拉网小调，喊着号子，胶东汉子的形象在这里体现得淋漓尽致

Chanting the rhythmical work songs while casting the fishing net—a vivid image of fishermen in Jiaodong Peninsula

Village. As one of the best preserved old villages in Jiaodc Peninsula, it is reputed to be the example of ecological fo houses and placed among the first of its kind on the Natio Traditional Village List for better protection.

The lotus-shaped village is surrounded by sea on its north, south and east sides. There is only one way leading to the continent. With a land area of 0.8 *square kilometers* it has 0.27 *square kilometers* of arable land. Its coastline is 10 *kilometers* long. There are around 200 households residing in this small village.

In the past centuries, villagers of Dongchudao lived peacefully on this beautiful small island. They made a living by fishing and farming. Local people respected *Mazu* as the patron goddess. The legend goes that during Wanli Period of the Ming Dynasty, several fishing boats sailing on the calm sea are confronted with a sudden furious wind storm. While the boats were near to being swept over by the violent waves, a quick lad thought of *Mazu* he once heard about from old people. He took the lead to kneel down on the prow followed by the crowd chanting "May *Mazu* bless us all···" In a moment, the wind storm died down, a streak of auspicious light running through the black clouds which dispersed and gave way to the sun and its golden rays. Those fishermen survived and returned safely with loads of fish. Then, people built a *Mazu* temple by the shore in honour of her kindness and protection. People in Dongchudao Village lived happily ever after, enjoying years of rich harvests.

So many years have passed and this place is full of memories for people who lived here. They are emotionally attached to the soil that nurtured this village. In order to make the future generations remember their origin, villagers built a Dongchudao Village Memorial Hall at the southwest corner of the village and inside the hall was a collection of a hundred used tools of previous villagers such as wooden boats, stone mills, ploughs, and seed ploughs. Walking into the hall, stories would come along with a fresh sea breeze, just like uncapping a jar of aged wine. Being geographically remote from urban areas, local villagers attach particular importance to education in the hope that their children can go out and experience more on the vast land. Earlier in 1936, with their income from selling scallops, villagers built Yuying Primary School which turned out to be the best village-based primary school in Rongcheng City. Actually, the Village Memorial Hall is where the school was once built.

Wandering on Isle Chu, visitors can see rows of seaweed houses that still keep the ancient features of simplicity and elegance. The gentle sea breeze carries along a fresh smell of fish and seagrass. With the flavors of the wildness of sea and a leisurely farming life, this northern fishing village has different scenes in four seasons. Sometimes, it is peaceful and tranquil with mild winds and waves like mellow clouds on a painting; while some other time, it becomes passionate and thunderous, showing off its tides and waves as if it is creating a majestic sketch. It is a place of endless inspirations for photographers and painters..

The most exotic scenes in the village are the seaweed houses in fuzzy "hats", the compactly thatched roofs that look like a fine fur coat protecting against the north winds. Representing local culture and customs, the cottages are rare precious eco-artworks. 80 out of the total 150 seaweed houses in the village have a history of one hundred years. Dongchudao Village is titled as a "Chinese Historical and Cultural Village" by the Ministry of Housing and Urban-Rural Development of China and the State Administration of Cultural Heritage, and it is also named "the Model Village of Rural Memories" by Shandong Province. There was a special coverage on the village in the travel documentary series called *Yuanfang de Jia* Season 2 (Homeland, Dreamland—Walking along the Chinese Coastline) created by China Central Television.

Most of the seaweed houses are quadrangle courtyards, single-yard *sanheyuan* (three-section compound house) or *siheyuan* (Chinese quadrangle). The gate is at the southeast corner and normally a screen wall was built behind the gate. There are three or four main rooms, adjoined by the east house and the west house. Built by rock blocks merging with each other and forming patterns randomly, the outer walls display the beauty of simplicity. Purlins and rafters of the house are made of wood, and interior walls are made of boards.

The thick tilted roof of the seaweed house resembles the hat of an ancient Chinese General in the Qing Dynasty, barely collecting any rainwater in its angle. The thatch covering is made of eelgrass, the unique wild seagrass growing nearby. Dried seaweed, containing large quantity of seawater bittern and colloid can be mothproof, resistant to mildew rot and non-flammable. Roofs made of such material can last for hundreds of years. Living in the house can be cozy since it is cool in the summer and warm in the winter.

The thatching of a roof is quite a study and craft which has been passed on from generation to generation. By piling up layers of seaweed and layers of straws alternatively, a thatched roof covering with lovely curve is built. Tiles and cement are used to build the ridge for guarding against strong winds. Finally, a chimney is added on the rooftop. At sunsets, the cooking smokes float lazily aloft and become a light fog drifting from the village to nearby shoreline, displaying an atmosphere of warmth and rural life.

The ridge of some thatched houses has collapsed after years of winds and rains and the seaweed, not much left, loosely covers the roof. Some houses have been renovated with cement and the sea-weed rooftops are replaced by bricks and tiles, losing their original features. Roaming down the mottled stone walkway is like travelling on the corridor of time. Rows of seaweed houses stand there silently and watch the coming and going of visitors. The few traces of the past are the hitching posts for horses standing by the walls, the blackboard news and slogans on the gables, reminding people of the bustling and peaceful old days.

Fortunately, wise villagers have realized the greatest fortune bestowed by ancestors despite the decline of traditional fishing industry and farming way of living. Houses are renovated in its original style along with road expansion and sanitation improvement. Adopted a conservation development strategy, the village is making efforts in the development of folk-custom tourism and advocating the fishing cultures and local customs. In addition, the village has established an International Seaweed House Arts Exchange Center, a Seaweed House Museum, a Sea View Gallery as well as a Tourist Service Center. Grain Rain Sea Festival, a yearly traditional cultural festival in Jiaodong Peninsula, attracts large numbers of tourists .An increasing number of visitors have travelled from afar to have a one-day experience of the local lifestyle – living in a seaweed house, tasting specialties at a fishing family, sleeping on the heated *kang* (a heatable brick bed in North China), getting along with the honest and hospitable locals while enjoying the magnificent landscape of the isle, the bay, the reefs and the stones.

By calling on any local household, you will enter into a single-yard *sanheyuan*. Through the long stone walkway leading to the north

house, the worn board wall of which has turned dark. On the left there is a briquette stove made of sun-dried mud bricks and piles of firewood. On the stove is a traditional cast-iron pan with a wooden lid which has been used for dozens of years. Except light bulbs and a small television, nothing in the house can be connected to the modern lifestyle. The landlord is more than 80 years old, he said, "It is left by my ancestors hundreds of years ago. I was born here. I have a special feeling towards it and I can't leave it." Such simple words express the nostalgia of the old man for his hometown, as well as the dedication of the older generation to the native culture. They are the spirit of Dongchudao Village.

^最后一道工序是将苫盖好的海草房表面再进行梳理，清理多余的杂草，将屋面修理得整整齐齐、顺溜光滑

The last step is to comb the thatched covering, removing surplus seaweed and straw and leaving the roof a smooth surface

< 修缮海草房时，房前屋后需要扎脚手架，地面、脚手架、房顶都要有人，草和泥要通过接力才能传递上去

Scaffold are needed around the house to thatch the roof. It requires the relay of people to pass the seaweeds and clay on the ground, the scaffold and the roof

< 人们习惯把腌制的咸菜、甜酱放到这大缸里进行储存，一缸咸菜可以吃上一年或更长时间

People usually store the pickled vegetables and sweet paste in big jars. One big jar of salted vegetables are enough for a year or longer

< 拖拉机是主要的运输工具，它源源不断地将海草从海边运到村里

Tractors are major means of transport in the village, carrying loads and loads of seaweed back home from the shore

^ 这些沉重的锚像一条条沉重的锁链，
牢牢地把渔民的命运拴在了船上

These heavy anchors, like chains, tied the fate of the fishermen firmly on the ships

^ 海是渔民的命根子，更是他们赖以生存的唯一依靠，他们在海上渔猎捕获，播种收割，祖祖辈辈就这样休养生息，世代相传，传承至今

The sea is vital to fishermen because their life depends on it. For generations, villagers have lived by fishing and farming

< 赶海拾贝在这里流传了几千年，与家人祖辈生长在海边，靠海吃海，大海的馈赠养育了他们，使他们一代代生息繁衍

Beachcombing for seashells is a tradition lasted for thousands of years. Generation that after generation, fishermen live by the sea and made a living out of it

07

烟墩角村

调查报告原文 / 摄影
毕延长

Reported / photograghed by
Bin Yanchang

> 渔船出海，上千只海鸥在船头盘旋，看来又是一个好兆头

The fishing vessel is sailing out with crowds of seagulls circling around, an auspicious omen

烟墩角是山东省荣成市俚岛镇的一个依山傍海、景色秀丽的小渔村。明朝时期倭寇经常骚扰我沿海地区，村里人就在村子东南方向的崮山之顶建了一座烽火墩。每当倭寇袭扰，村民就点燃烽火通驻守官兵歼击来犯之敌，烟墩角村由此得名。明崇祯年间，曲氏家族从荣成市港西镇巍巍村迁居于至今已有近 400 年，现有居民约 600 户，祖祖辈辈以打鱼为生。

沿着舒缓的山坡爬到崮山顶，只见一个十几米高的烽火墩遗址躺在那里。举目眺望，东面是浩渺黄海，波光粼粼；俯视脚下，峭壁临海而立，浪花拍打礁石，轰然作响；东北极目之处是中国的好望角——天尽头；西北就是烟墩角村。

作为曾经的边防卫所，烟墩角村虽然带着古战场的硝烟之气，却是中国少有的人与自然和谐共生乐园。这里南面朝海，东、西方地势较高，中间地势凹陷，形似一个聚宝盆。走进村庄，仿佛进入童话世

瓦绿树，天鹅在自由翱翔，扇贝在清净的浅海里爬行，炊烟袅袅掩不住鸡鸣犬吠，重重屋檐处还可看到白帆点点。2015 年元旦，中国中央电视台就在烟墩角村前的天鹅湾出海口向全界直播了“新年第一缕阳光”，英国 BBC 也曾在这里取景拍摄过纪录片。

烟墩角村有三宝：海草房、天鹅湾和中华海上第一奇石——花斑彩石。海草房起源于汉，到了明清时，海草房已经成为胶东半岛流传最广的民居样式。渔民们以厚石砌墙，用石勾勒出红、黄、黑色灰缝，其古朴典雅的门楼上，飞檐翘瓦传递着东方的灵气；院门口影壁上大的“福”字，为小院增添祥和安乐。海草房就地取材、美观实用，完全符合当地渔民的日常活起居特点，已被列为山东省非物质文化遗产。

让烟墩角村声名远播的是，这里有世界上最大的天鹅越冬乐园，是这种自然精灵的福地。

^矗立在村中央广场的村碑记录着烟墩角村的发展文化

The "Village Stone Tablet" standing in the middle of the square has witnessed the development of Yandunjiao Village

“双翮凌长风，须臾万里逝”，天鹅在东西方文化里都是纯洁、美丽、高贵的象征。

烟墩角村的东边有一座小山拦住黄海，形成一湾宁静的海港。其海水清澈见底，金色的阳光在浪花上跳跃；两侧各有一条淡水小溪流入，带来新鲜活水；丰富的鱼虾和浮游生物在水底遨游，让天鹅在寒冷的冬天也有充足的食物。每年 11 月到次年 4 月，上万只来自西伯利亚和新疆的天鹅飞抵这里，在碧波荡漾的海湾里自在游弋，如一群白衣仙子降临凡间，让人恍兮惚兮，不知是何方仙境。

数百年来，纯朴善良的村民们已经习惯了这些每年光临的客人并把它们当成村子的一员。烟墩角在每只天鹅的生命旅途中，也已不再是一个普通驿站，而是恋恋不舍的家乡吧。

烟墩角村的神奇之处还在于村东南海面上的一块奇特的石头。隔海相望，这块巨石上赤、橙、黄、白、青相互交融，白天在阳光的照射下闪闪发亮，夜晚在灯光的映衬中绚丽多彩，当地人称它为花斑彩石。传说它是当年女娲补天遗漏的神石，又名女娲靴，被誉为中华海上第一奇石，在清朝道光年间就是荣成八景之一。据考证，此石为 5 亿多年前火山岩浆喷发而成，由于长期受海水的侵蚀形成五彩花斑，是远古留给现代的奇观。

近观彩石，初看淡雅恬静，再看神韵万象。那花纹似描似绣、似铸似雕、似削似劈。在凹进去的正

上，不同颜色的线条形成不同图案，如庄严佛像，似嫦娥舞袖，如枝叶繁茂，似金蝉灵猴……海浪这位天然的雕塑大师，用亿万年创作周期，完成了这妙不可言的作品。

烟墩角村以花斑彩石为主景点，还开发了包括奇石馆、文物馆、书画馆、藏书馆等景观的综合旅游区。由于地势便利，村办企业也较多，烟墩角村是胶东有名的富裕村庄。改革开放初期，村民们一度大力改造海草房，有的换成了砖瓦，有的推倒盖起楼房，另外，随着近海养殖的增多和捕捞业发展，海草越来越少，价格越来越高，于是，传统海草房有日渐式微之势。

随着旅游业的发展，乡亲们逐渐接受了文物保护的理念，对保护原生态景观以及发展民俗旅游做出了长远规划。这些数百年的传统民居不但不会退出历史舞台，还会经过更人性化的升级改造，继续传承下去。

近几年来，造访此地的游客越来越多，村里还出现了渔家乐、天鹅之家等民俗旅店。屋舍虽小却连接着八方游客。一到冬天，更有大批摄影爱好者追寻白天鹅的足迹来到这里，他们欣赏着“成倾胡天碧，一池雪花白”的美景，深深沉浸在众生喜乐、物我两忘的氛围中。

辽阔悠远的天空下，在这块东方极地上，自然之美、动物之美、民俗之美恰到好处地融为一体，形成了一个动静皆宜、天人合一的俗世天堂。

Yandunjiao Village

Yandunjiao Village is a pleasing fishing village in Lidao, a town in Rongcheng City, Shangdong Province. It is located by the sea against the hills with beautiful scenery. During the Ming Dynasty, people living in coastal villages were frequently harassed by Japanese pirates. The villagers, hence, built a beacon tower at the top of a hill called Gu to the southeast of the village. Once the invaders approached, people would light the tower up to inform the stationed army and they would come and fight the enemy. That's how it was named Yandunjiao (mound of smoke) Village. During the Chongzhen Period of the Ming Dynasty, almost 400 years ago, the Qu family came and settled from Weiwei Village, Gangxi Town, Rongcheng. Currently, there are 600 households in the village and for generations they have largely depended on fishing to make a living.

Climbing up Mount Gu at its peak, you'll see the relics of the beacon tower, which is ten plus *meters* high, lying desolate. Looking out into the distance, you can see the water shining in the vast Yellow Sea to the east; down the cliff, you can hear the waves thundering against the rocks; to its northeast it's the End of Heaven – China's Cape of Good Hope; and Yandunjiao Village lies right to its northwest.

Once a frontier defense, the village still keeps the bearing of an ancient war field, but now it is one of the few known tourist attractions where people and nature can live together harmoniously. The village lies in a basin, with its east and west rising above, its south facing the sea and the middle sunken into the ground. Walking into the village, it's like entering the world of fairy tales. You'll see red roofs and green plots of vegetables here and there, trees and reeds swaying in the wind, swans flying in the clear sky, and seashells moving around in the shoals. There are households whose cooking smoke spiraling upward from the chimneys, and in the yard the crowing of cocks is competing with the barking of dogs. Beyond the rows of houses, white spots of sails are scattered on the sea. In 2015, on the New Year's Day China Central Television (CCTV) broadcasted live to the world the first glimpse of sunshine of the year from Swan Bay port by the edge of Yandunjiao Village. The BBC also once filmed a documentary here.

^太阳的光芒照射在渔村，海草、绿树、红瓦，古老的村落焕发出青春的活力

The golden sunshine falls on the village, to the seaweed houses, trees and red tiles. The old village is glowing with vigor

There are three treasures in Yandunjiao, the seaweed house, the Swan Bay and Huaban Caishi – the rarest stone on China's sea waters. Seaweed houses date back to the Qin and the Han Dynasties. Back in the Ming and the Qing Dynasties, seaweed houses were the most popular folk residence on Jiaodong Peninsula. Fishermen built the walls of the house with thick rocks, caulking the cracks between the rocks in red, yellow and black with lime. Above the simple, elegant style gate, the cornice and tiles display the oriental spirit. It's hard not to notice the big Chinese character Fu on the screen wall which adds a sense of peace and happiness to the family. The roof of the house, made from local seaweeds and straws, is aesthetically attractive and practical to the lifestyle of local households. Seaweed houses are included in the provincial category of intangible cultural heritage.

What makes Yandunjiao Village popular is that it is the world's largest swan paradise. In winters, swans will gather here and enjoy themselves, spreading their wings and flying high up in the sky and in a moment disappearing in sight. Both Eastern and Western cultures share the cultural connotation of this elegant creature as purity, beauty and nobility.

To the east of Yandunjiao Village stands a hill which blocks the view of the Yellow Sea. The bay becomes a quiet place where golden sunshine often plays with the sparkling sprays on the crystal clear surface. Fresh water is introduced by creeks nearby, nurturing numerous fish and plankton which feed thousands of swans from Siberia and Xinjiang each year staying for winter months from November to April. The big birds congregate around the bay, craning their necks and singing to the sky, dancing as they taking-off and landing on the water with outspread wings or chasing after each other like a group of fairies-in-white from heaven. People might not help themselves in imaging a wonderland in front of their eyes. In the last hundred several hundred years, honest and hospitable villagers have been used to tourists coming each year. They are friendly to the visitors like treating familiar neighbours. For the swans, Yandunjiao is not a winter station in their lifelong journey, but home they'd be reluctant to leave.

< 独特的样式，独特的建筑，独特的门楼，灰色的瓦，两头向上挑，俗称挑翅子门楼

The house is unique in style and structure. The gate, with a roof in grey tiles, is called "Tiaochizi" for its upswept ridge ends

One of the wonders of Yandunjiao Village is the rare stone sitting on the sea to its southeast. From a distance, the rock looks five colours – red, orange, yellow, white and blue; shining in the golden radiations of the sun while in the evening it becomes even more gorgeous reflected by the water; hence, it is called Huaban Caishi (spotted stone). There is a legend that it is a wonder stone which was left over by Nuwa (a goddess in ancient Chinese mythology) when she repaired the heaven, and people called it "Nuwa Boot". It is dubbed the number one rare stone in China's sea waters. In the Qing Dynasty, it was one of the eight Rongcheng scenic spots. According to research, it is formed by lava of a volcano erupted over 500 million years ago. The five-colored spots are due to the erosion of sea water. It is a wonderful gift from the ancient time. There is also a poem about the rock and the meaning is: "a thousand years in making, out of sea emerged the spotted rock; surprised at it, people came to take pictures. " The villagers are happy that it has turned into such a hot tourist destination.

An up-close look at the stone you can feel its tranquility and elegance, and the longer you observe it gets more unpredictably charming. The patterns on the rock bear the resemblance to paintings, embroidery, casting, and carving, cutting or hacking. Formed by lines of different colors, some of the patterns look like solemn Buddha statues, some in the shape of dancing Chang'e (the Chinese goddess of the Moon), and some a flourishing tree or a savvy monkey...Thanks to the waves, the master of nature who crafted this unequalled work over millions of years.

Yandunjiao Village has become a comprehensive tourist attraction with the promotion of Huaban Caishi and the establishment of the Wonder Stone Museum, Historical Relics Museum, Painting and Calligraphy Museum and Library. Due to easy transportation, dozens of village-run enterprises have made Yandunjiao a rich village known in Jiaodong area. At the beginning of the reform and opening-up, people made great efforts in reconstruction of seaweed houses, turning them into brick-and-tile houses or buildings, and villagers became almost no different from city residents. With the rapid development of offshore aquaculture and fishery, the quantity of seaweed declines and the price went higher and higher. As a result, traditional seaweed houses were gradually abandoned.

Thanks to the development of tourism, the notion of the preservation of historical relics became increasingly popular among the villagers. They started to protect the primitive ecological landscape and make long-term plans for the development of folk custom tourism. These hundreds-of-years-old houses will not disappear; instead, they will be revamped to upgraded practical uses in the future.

In recent years, more and more visitors came to enjoy the beautiful scenery of the village. A few folk inns in such styles as fishing house or home of swan appeared. Although small, these dwellings accommodated tourists from various places. In the winter, a large number of swan photographers came to indulge themselves to the stunning scenery of snow white flying fairies dancing against the backdrop of the blue sky and sea.

Under the vast sky, the beauty of the nature, creatures and folk customs have come perfectly together on this amazing oriental land. It is like a worldly heaven that holds the balance between vivacity and tranquility, achieving the harmony between human and nature.

< “瞧！爸爸妈妈下海还没有回来。”这就是渔家的生活

“Look! Dad and mom go fishing in the sea and they are not at home yet.” This is the daily life scene of fishing families

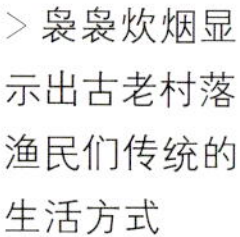

> 袅袅炊烟显示出古老村落渔民们传统的生活方式

The smoke from chimneys shows the traditional lifestyle of fishing households in this old village

> 百年海草房错落有致形成“驼峰”

These old seaweed houses are properly arranged in the village like the humps of camels

海带养殖井然有序，作业的船只返航收工

Seaweed planting is well-organized. The working vessels are sailing back home

< 海带是村里的一大特产，渔民们将收上来的海带进行加工：将根部宽大的部分加工装箱，销往全国；将末梢部分加工成海带丝；将下脚料加工成饲料用来喂养鲍鱼

Seaweed is the major specialty of the village. Once harvested, the seaweed will be processed. The ones with fat root will be boxed for sale nationwide; the tips will be made as seaweed shreds and the rest be used to feed the abalone

> 有5亿年前的花斑彩石悄然屹立在村南的海中，经过海水这位雕琢师的精心打磨形成了五彩花斑，衍生出许多神话传说

Being five hundred million years old, the Huaban Caishi stands quietly in the sea facing the south of the village. Years of cutting and polishing by the waves gave the stone five-colored spots, which are picturesque patterns of myths and legends

> 顶天立地的渔民汉子，独自驾船出海作业

A self-dependent and fearless fisherman is working on the sea alone

> 静静的港湾，静静的渔船，它们经历了大海的咆哮、风浪的袭击，本该有一个安静的港湾歇息歇息，渔船在深思沉默，海水在静静地诉说

Fishing boats are lying still on the quiet bay. The boats, survived the rough sea and ferocious waves, should have been entitled to rest at a gentle harbor. Now the boats are contemplating and the sea is whispering

08

里箬村

调查报告原文 / 摄影
郭浩

Reported / photograghed by
Guo Hao

> 俯瞰里箬

A bird's-eye view of
Liruo Village

半山石屋赛琼阁

“千户石屋鱼鳞叠，半住山腰半水滨”，300 年前，来自福建的陈氏一族在浙江省温岭市石塘镇的处山海交接的区域发现了一方乐土。定居下来的人们打鱼为业、繁衍生息，一座又一座石头房子像山冒出的竹笋，渐渐将山坡覆盖，因“有山焉，层层包裹，故曰箬。又分内外两层，故曰外箬里箬”。里箬村西、北三面临海，地处箬山内侧，故名里箬村。

村内的石屋之间由一条主道贯通，石阶从村口铺到村尾，纵横交错。石屋规模小一点的，呈一字排列；规模大些的，形成合院式院落。民居风格总体上是朴素的，但也透着南方人的巧思和情趣。厚的墙体格外结实，就像汉子有力的肩膀，支撑起整个村子的骨架。墙头装饰着砖砌漏窗，绿釉花砖的隔使敦实的平面产生横竖、虚实、光影、色调的变化，打破空间的闭塞，产生了移步易景的效果。还有巧雅致的石花窗镶嵌在石墙上，如同画廊里挂着的一幅幅民俗画。

更可喜的是，家家户户的阳台上常摆放着一盆盆鲜花，红红白白黄黄，是主人精心打理日的雅趣。拾级而上，花花草草在路边点缀。路过院落，沁人心脾的花香溢满小径，就连院子里，不忘砌一个花台，或者因陋就简地在泡沫箱里栽上盆景。合着远处的蓝天碧海，此情此景让恍若置身于爱琴海边的小镇。一座典型的合院由进门、正房、左右厢房及外墙围合而成，占约 200 平方米。院门一般有两道，一道开在东北角，一道开在西北侧。正房为两层小楼，三开间，平整厚实的石块砌筑。外墙用不规则毛石垒砌，厚约 0.5 米。这样的石屋坚固妥帖，和山坡然一体，又防暑保温，冬暖夏凉。午后坐在门口的石阶上远望渔船风帆，沙鸥翔集，是村民一大乐事。

里箬村最著名的建筑要数金涯尾路 39 号西侧的陈和隆旧宅，它被列为浙江省级文物保护单位。这是一座规模宏大的宅院，被石板路分为前后两部分。东墙上嵌有一块《陈氏卜园记》石碑，为清光绪年间举人顾歧所撰，记载建宅始末。宅院前面有两幢楼，东侧楼名海滨庐，又称旭升楼，民国十七年（1928 年）建。楼门框上镌刻着“沧海列层楼堪为蛟龙栖息，青山多古意聊容卧虎藏身”的楹联。楼底层为地下仓库，面海开有水门，涨潮时货船可直接泊到屋内卸货。楼前有近百平方米的观海凉台，其门框、石柱、栏板上有描绘着海洋生物的精美石刻，后面部分有楼房 7 间，前楼与后楼之间有飞桥相通，显示着大户人家的不凡气派。

原宅主陈和隆“三世经营航运得宜”而富甲一方,于是造起了这座冠绝一时的宅第。“设施得宜，遂觉草有忘忧之意，花含解语之容，鱼多情而听琴，鸟识趣而逐酒”，成为这座海边渔村的盛景。

除了石屋、石窗、石阶，里箬村最出名的就是大奏鼓了。这是一种古老的庆丰收、祭海神的舞蹈，由福建惠安渔民从闽南传来。它在异乡石塘扎下了根，并被列入国家非物质文化遗产名录，但在故乡福建已销声匿迹。每年元宵节，大奏鼓巡游成为当地渔民一年中最热闹的记忆。“男扮女装”是它的特色，叔叔伯伯们抹上白粉，腮涂胭脂，耳挂金耳环，手戴金手镯，脚套金脚镯，脑后扎上羊角发髻，逗得孩子们笑得前仰后合。宝蓝绲金鱼纹边的短褂，合着大海和阳光的明媚色调，伴随着铙钹锣鼓，喧闹出一片喜庆。

正月一过，青壮年纷纷外出，村里就剩下一些留守老人。老人，是一个村子的灵魂。走近他们，倾听他们的故土往事、他们的暮年神思，就能触摸到一个村落的灵魂深处。

村里石道蜿蜒起伏，老人们腿脚不便，总要拄着什么上下石阶。但是他们的脸上总是挂着安详的微笑，一点不累。黄昏、古道、夕阳下，拄着拐杖在青石板路上慢悠悠前行的奶奶，抽着烟远眺的爷爷，大概是游子们最眷恋的故乡画面吧。

穿过石道，走进普通人家的石屋，满眼皆是用了约莫十来年的老物件，泛着黄色的旧时光味道。新农村建设之后，旧屋里有了现代化的一切。人，却突然孤独了。老奶奶依旧穿着旧式的布褂大衣，梳着老式发髻，依旧把小院拾掇得井井有条，红色的盆桶，竹竿上晾晒的衣服，绿油油的花木，一切都极为妥当，仿若这平静的岁月独自流淌。

老人们都是七八十岁的年纪，常年的劳作使他们的身板硬朗。他们对游客毫不见外，一位老奶奶说，家门口的这块石板上，她一坐就是 50 多年，最初她还是一个 20 岁出头的姑娘。

窗沿上的“福娃”是过年时留下的，现已褪色了许多。年过了，儿孙们也就散了，留下老两口，坐着、等着、守着。随处可见的晾衣架上，有时挂着小孩的衣服，那是属于上小学的孙辈甚至重孙辈的，他们也是留守老人跟出外打工的儿女们最紧密的联系。

年轻人中也有子承父业的。在儿子接替了出海工作后，老人便清闲下来。每当夕阳西下的时候，老人便会一个人来到临海的石屋露台上，望着远方海面上进进出出的

^孤独的古村村民

A solitary old villager

渔船，沉默许久。似是回忆，似是向往。人生如海浪，涨涨落落。老人说年轻时候他和大海搏斗，靠大海讨生活，却不懂大海。到老了，终于懂了。

寂寥的老村是里箬悠长的背景音乐，不远处的渔港是旋律上跳动的音符，在这里可窥见里箬村生生不息的生命力。码头引桥一端连着陆地，一端连着大海；一边是货车，一边是渔船。

为了保证捕捞的海产品的新鲜，船一靠岸，港口上的人们便忙碌起来。在旁观者看来狭窄的引桥，却承担着搬运货物的重任。沉重的步伐一遍又一遍踏在桥面上，狭窄的通道洒满了渔民的汗水，让人看着一阵惊险，却不禁为他们完美的配合叫好。货物搬运上岸后，就是装车、打包工作。汉子们光着膀子，裸露着健壮的肌肉，弯腰、起身、举臂、扛起，一气呵成。虽然紧张得没有喘息之机，这充满鱼腥味的画面里却满是欢声笑语。半天之后，一堆货物高高耸起，他们会抽上一支烟，穿上时髦的牛仔裤，戴上腕表，有的进城约会，有的回家和父母妻儿团聚，吃上一口热腾腾的渔家饭。这就是普通里箬人的一天，他们用双手创造财富，因为是里箬人，所以热爱大海。

夕阳西下，渔船安详地停泊在港湾，水面漾着碎金，船体上贴着“一帆风顺”的祝词。无论海上还是陆地，现实与梦想，都能让人感受到一种乐观、诗意的精神沉淀在里箬人的日子深处。

渔港新貌

New look of the local harbor

Liruo Village

"Hundreds of stone houses stack together like fish scales, with half lying on the mountainside and the other half by the sea." 300 years ago, the Chen family, which originated in Fujian Province, discovered this land of promise at the crossing of sea and mountain at Shitang County of Wenling City in Zhejiang Province. They live here for generations, fishing and building one stone house after another, which gradually covered the mountainside. The village towers the inner side of Mountain Ruo, thus the name of Liruo Village (meaning the inner side of mountain Ruo in Chinese).

One main road connects the stone houses and stone steps zigzag through the entire village, forming a grid-like structure like a fishing net. Stone houses of smaller sizes stand in lines, whereas the ones of larger scales form a circular court. These houses are simple yet still show a hint of creativity and of the delight toward life of the southern people of China. Thick and solid walls, like a strong man, shoulder the entire fishing village. The top of the walls are decorated with brick traceries and green glazed tiles in alternative fashion, which offers changes between the horizontal level and vertical level of the building, lights and shadows, as well as colors. The design breaks the space limitation and creates the effect of view change as the viewer moves. Even the stonewalls are decorated with delicate lattice windows, like lines of folk paintings hanging in the gallery.

More pleasantly, local residents have the tradition of placing potted flowers on their balconies. These colorful flowers show the residents' elegant taste in life and beauty. Walking on the stone steps and admiring the grass and flowers, one cannot help but be embraced by the refreshing fragrance. Within the yard, there might be a garden, or at least some potted plants in foam box in the most simplistic manner. Staying in the village, with the scenery of the blue sky and sea, one might think he is living in a Greek village by the Aegean Sea.

The local circular court, typically formed by two doors, the main house and two flank rooms and the external walls, is about 200 *square meters*. The doors are placed on the northeastern and northwestern corners. The main house of two floors and three bays is built with flat and solid stones. The external walls are built with rubble stones and are about 0.5 *meters* wide. The stone houses stand firmly on the mountainside. The house keeps itself cool in summer and warm in winter. Local residents spend their afternoons by sitting on the steps in front of their gates and enjoying the view of fishing boat and seagulls.

The most famous building in Liruo Village is the former residence of Chen Helong, which is located on the west side of No. 39 Jinyawei Road. The mansion, listed as a cultural relic at the Zhejiang Provincial Level, is divided into a frontcourt and a backcourt by a stone road. The eastern wall is embedded with a stone stele, namely The Story of Buyuan of the Chen Family written by Gu Qi, a famous scholar during the reign of Emperor Guangxu of the Qing Dynasty. The stele records the history of the residence from the beginning. In the front of the residence, there are two buildings, with the one on the east, called Haibinlu or Xushenglou being built in 1928. The door frame is engraved with a couplet "By the sea lies the mansion where the dragon lives, on the mountainside lies the relics where the tiger crouches." The warehouse is situated beneath the mansion, with a door open to the sea, which facilitates the boats to unload inside when the tides run high. In front of the mansion is a view deck, which is about 100

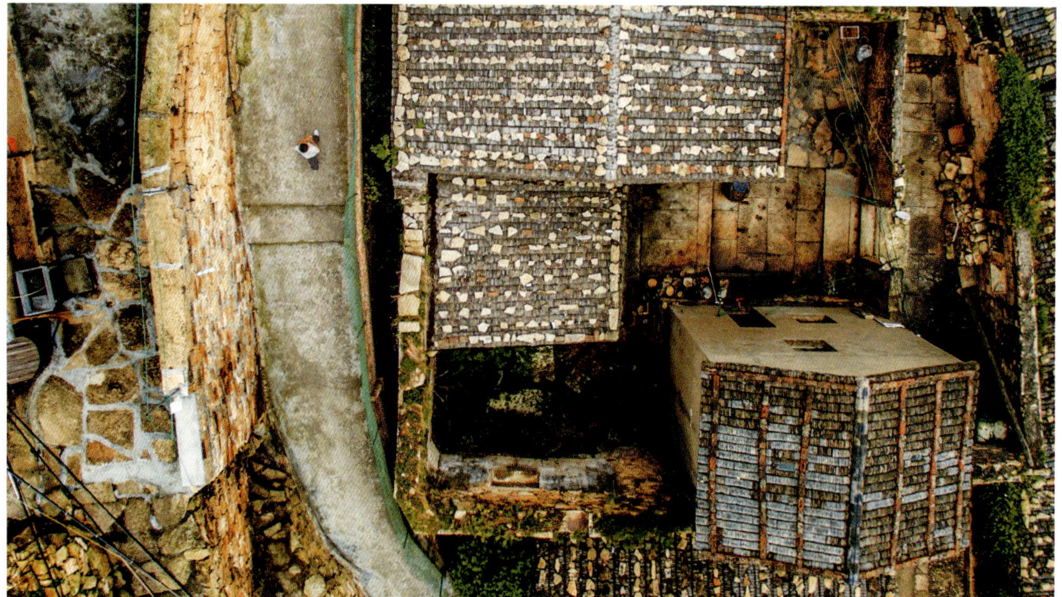

^俯瞰里箬

A bird's-eye view of Liruo Village

square meters, with exquisite cravings of sea creatures on the doorframes, columns and fences. The building in the back courts has seven rooms. There is a bridge to connect the two buildings in the front and back courts, showing the extravagant life style of the Chen Family.

Former owner Chen Helong built a fortune from shipping and also this magnificent mansion. "Finely equipped mansion, where its lovely grasses and flowers help you forget all the sorrows, its fish and birds know the music and wine." The mansion has become an attraction in the village.

Besides its construction, Liruo Village is also well known for *dazougu*, a traditional dance to celebrate the harvest and pay tribute to the Sea God. The fishermen in Huian, Fujian Province from Minnan, passed on the dance. Though it is no longer seen in Fujian Province, the dance is rooted in Liruo Village and listed in the National Intangible Cultural Heritage List. For the local fishermen, *dazougu* parade in Chinese Lantern Festival has became the jolliest memory of local fishermen. "Men dressed up as women" is *dazougu's* special feature, with men wearing heavy makeups, jewelries and having their hair pulled back in two funny buns, which makes children laugh. The dancing man, wearing traditional short blue jacket trimmed with goldfish-like lines, put on a wonderful show together with cheerful music under the bright sun by the seaside.

At the end of the Chinese lunar New Year, young people leave Liruo for work and the elderly stay behind. They are the spirit of this village. If you could approach them, listen to their stories and thoughts, you would get closer to understanding the spirit of Liruo.

The stone steps zigzag through the village. The elderly would have to use canes to move up and down, however their smiling faces never show any tiredness. It always touches the softest spots of anyone from Liruo who travels away from home to think of the sight of grandmother hobbling on the stone steps and grandfather staring afar and smoking at dusk.

Entering any house in the village through stone steps, what you would see are the items which have been used for over a decade and are worn. After the wave to build the new countryside, people in Liruo started to enjoy the convenience of modern life; yet, all of sudden, people feel the loneliness. Old granny stays in the stone house, wearing a traditional bun in a retro-looking jacket, and still does the laundry, as well as the gardening to make sure everything in the house is neat and clean. Time drifts away so peacefully.

The elderly make visitors feel at home in Liruo. The old people in Liruo are in their 70s' or 80s' and are still strong from years' of work. One granny tells her story of sitting on the very same stone for 50 years since she was 20.

Fuwa artifacts standing on the windowsill are from last year and their colors have started to fade. After Chinese Lunar New Year, children and grandchildren leave home one after another, leaving the old couples at home, sitting, waiting and expecting. From time to time, you might see children's clothes hanging on the hangers. The clothes might be the couple's grandchildren's or great grandchildren's. Kids are the closest link between left-behind old people and their children who leave home and work as migrant workers.

After knocking, we came to visit an old man. After his son took over the job of sea fishing, the old man retired. At sunset, he would come on the stone balcony to watch the fishing boat coming in and out of dock. He was in silence, half recollecting, and half longing. The tide of life! The old man told us he never truly understood the sea while he was battling for life and trying to earn a living back when he was young. Now he does.

If we could compare Liruo Village to a piece of music, the solitary old village would be the mellow background music, while the nearby harbor would be the beating notes over the melody. One would touch the never-ending vitality of Liruo Village from here. The bridge at the harbor connects the land and the sea, as well as the fishing boats and trucks.

To ensure the freshness of the sea products, once the boat comes ashore, workmen on the harbor start to get busy with their work. The seemly arrow bridge approach actually shoulders enormous weight. Busy feet thump on the bridge and the narrow approach is wetted by fishermen's sweat. Though it might seem quite dangerous, one cannot help being impressed by their seamless cooperation. After the cargos are carried ashore, they still need to be packed and loaded onto the truck. The workmen would stretch their strong muscular arms and carry the cargo with their hands and shoulders. The work is busy and intense, but people fill it with laughter. After half a day, the cargo towers on the dock. The workmen would feel relaxed after smoking some cigarettes. They would change into fancy clothes and some might go on a date, others would return home to their family for a warm dinner. This is a typical day for people in Liruo Village. They build their fortune by their own hands. They say, as the sons of Liruo, they love the sea.

At sunset, fishing boats berth peacefully at bay, with a couplet "everything goes well" sticking on the sides. The waves are tinted with a touch of gold. Whether on the sea or land, in reality or dream, one would feel the cheerful and poetic spirit rooted in the life of people in Liruo Village.

∨俯瞰里箬

A view of Liruo Village

08 里箬村
Liruo
Village

^俯瞰里箬

A view of Liruo Village

\/> 孤独古村

The solitary ancient village

09

走马塘村

调查报告原文 / 摄影
胡寒

Reported / photograghed by
Hu Han

> 中新屋大院群

Zhongxinwu Courtyard Complex

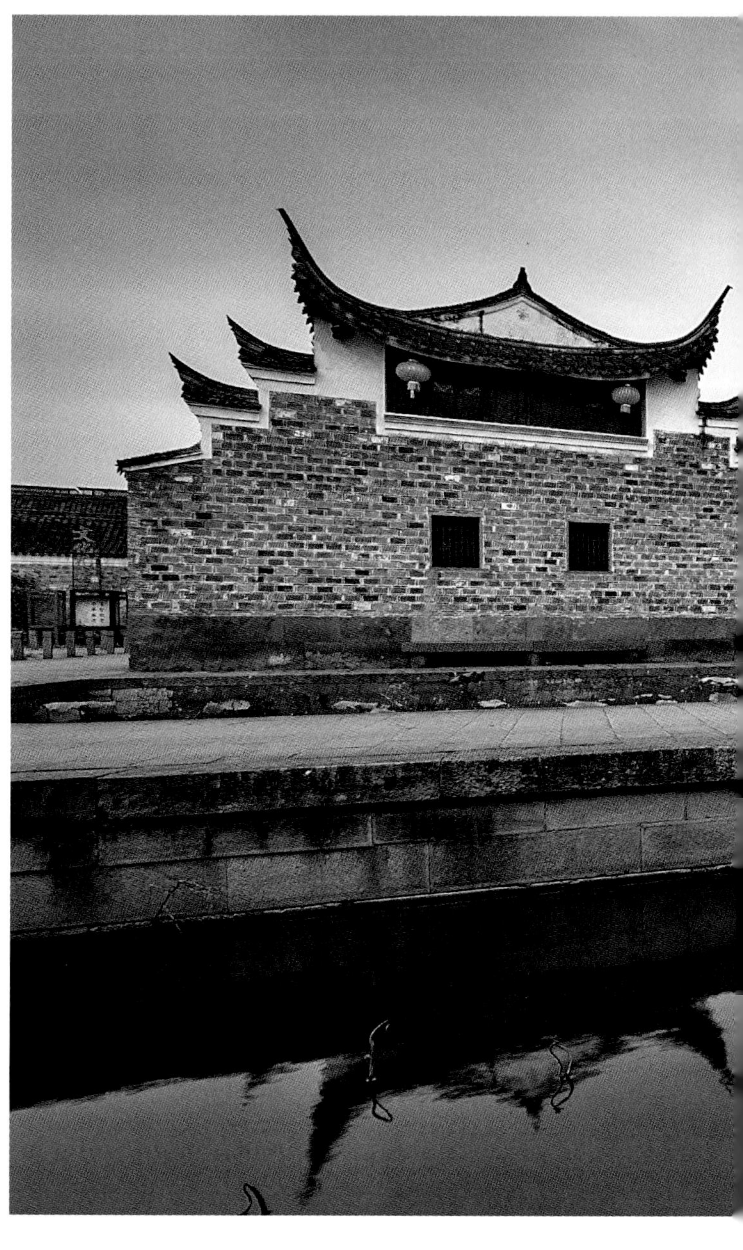

曲苑风荷驻马蹄

浙江自古就是物华天宝、人杰地灵之地，这里采莲、浣纱的场景以及梅子酒、线装书等物件都是典的江南符号，浮动着一代代才子佳人的动人传说。浙东的鄞南平原上就卧着这样一个古村，村子里清古建众多，民风淳朴。更令人叫绝的是村里出过 76 名进士、111 名国学生以及朝官加地方官 155 留有“一门四尚书，父子两侍郎，祖孙三学士”的佳话，被誉为中国进士第一村。这就是宁波市鄞州区山镇走马塘村，被赞为“四明古郡，文献之邦，有江山之胜，水陆之饶”。现全村共有 1500 余人，皆为陈

据史载，走马塘村始建于北宋太宗端拱年间， 明州知府陈矜之子为父守陵，携带家眷定居于此，今已传 38 代。在这期间，陈氏后裔无论官位多高，返还故里一律遵循“文官下轿，武官下马，徒步进村的祖训，走马塘由此而得名。

走马塘村由 2 个自然村落组成，面积约 2 平方千米。现存明代建筑 8 处，清代建筑比比皆是，另

幢建于民国时期具有西洋风格的建筑。独特的水系是这里的一大特色。全村由 4 条河流环抱，来桥、西沈桥、庆丰桥等跨于河上；东邻漕、邵家漕、蟹肚脐、后王漕、徐家漕散落其间，还10 余个大小参差不齐的小池藏于村中。这套水利系统设计巧妙，能聚能排，形成了流畅的网疏通系统，确保全村免遭旱涝火灾的侵袭。

想象中，这样的古村应该是雕梁画栋的翰林府第、山水如画的通灵宝境，但眼前的走马村却是田野中一个平实、简朴的乡野村落。这里不适合呼朋引伴来凑热闹，更适合信步缓行，静品味。

穿过村口的进士村石牌坊，穿过民国年间设计修建的紫来桥，那些歪斜衰败的砖木老屋发着历史的味道。轻烟朦胧，小巷幽幽，马头墙的飞檐挑角似刺破蓝天。

村里最大的建筑群叫中新屋大院群，位于村落东北隅，建于清乾隆年间，整片建筑共 432 间房，占地约 4000 平方米，数十户人家共享 5 个天井。廊轩层层，甬道纵横，无论从哪一间出发，都能绕到所有房间。下雨天在这个大院里穿行不需要撑伞。走出院门，迎面是约 2 亩的荷花池，两座拱桥横跨南北，“出淤泥而不染”的荷花是走马塘陈氏的族花。每到初夏，荷花盛开，亭亭玉立，水面倒映着房舍飞檐，如一幅工笔水乡画。

走马塘村现存的老街并不长，大约二三十米，原是姜山至奉化等地的必经之路，在清代中晚期已成规模。老街东西走向，石板路面宽约 5 米。店铺多为二层楼房，砖木结构。底层临街为商店，二层住宿。在鼎盛时期，每逢市集，埠头挤满船只，街上熙来攘往。奉化莼湖的海鲜、茅山的竹木、斗门桥的鱼虾、走马塘的菱藕，以及乡下的瓜果蔬菜，在各个商铺门口码得成捆成堆。南货店、酒馆、米店、银楼、客栈等大小商号鳞次栉比。每年五月二十五日还有稻花会，到了晚上，家家户户在街上摆起祭桌，整条街灯火通明，热闹非凡。

顺路前行，一条石板小径引领游客踏进走马塘村的核心——蟹肚脐。这是一方不大的池子，却是连接内外水系的终端。其三面有石堤围绕，方便船只停泊；若干石阶穿凿其间，供村民洗涮、船家上岸。河水倒映着粉墙黛瓦、木格窗棂，间或有妇女洗衣激荡起的水花打散图案。一棵千年古树横卧河面，树枝苍劲，树冠葱郁。不知哪位才子给这湾碧水起了蟹肚脐的名，既有古村中心之意，又有游子返乡回到宗室怀抱之情。那些漫长的赶考岁月里，多少年轻人从这里出发，背井离乡，追求他们光宗耀祖的理想。

在蟹肚脐西侧，静立着一座寂寥的小院，门上覆满金银花药草。这是贻谷堂，人称陈半仙的民国鄞南名医陈松涛的私人诊所。走马塘村有 3 个“百年”——百年诊所、百年消防、百年学堂。百年消防的消防设备赠给了上海有关部门，百年学堂现在是一所现代小学，唯有百年诊所贻谷堂还是古色古香。院内的地面上刻有一枚很大的圆形钱币，钱币中间的孔洞里有一朵盛开的白莲花浮雕，园内遍植阶前草及四时花木，沾衣留香。

^ 老街棋牌房

A chess and card room on an ancient street

绕过村子西南角的陈氏祠堂走到村边，一条清亮的小河出现在眼前，这就是君子河，取意“先生塘隐先生柳，君子河开君子花”。陈氏以耕读传家，门风极正，“君子”两字寄托着祖先对子孙的期盼。北宋嘉祐八年（1063 年），吏部侍郎陈谧告老还乡，一叶扁舟千里漂泊，父老乡亲夹岸相迎。两只沉甸甸的木箱被抬上岸来，众人以为是雪花白银，打开一看却是厚实的半旧书册。后人赞道“尘埃满匣空鸣剑，风雨归舟只载书”。陈氏一族千百年来文脉不绝的缘由可见一斑。

陈氏祠堂北面住宅的东墙，有一处极为精美的石窗，学者将其命名为浙南石窗。石窗图案大都围绕驱邪、平安、招财、祈福的主题。人物图案有八仙中的张果老、蓝采和、吕洞宾等；图案有“福”“乾”等吉祥文字。石窗雕花镂空，质地古朴，研磨精细，开闭自如，和木窗并无两样。环顾四周，雕梁、画栋、飞檐随处可见。气势恢宏的五马墙分 5 个飞檐，次第上升，雕有许多精美的图案。明清时期等级森严，只有位极人臣的官宦之家才可建造这样的宅第。

走马塘村还有一座私人档案馆，保存着与村落相关的字画、照片、报刊等书籍及牌匾等珍贵资料达万件以上。档案馆的主人并非陈氏后裔，而是当年来此插队的知青，他返乡后仍对走马塘村念念不忘。2005 年，他回到这个魂牵梦萦的第二故乡，开始收集与走马塘村有关的文物、资料，包括全国各地书画家以走马塘村为主题创作的作品，包括名家为 76 位进士画的画像。还有千年历史的普安寺“南来第一山”匾额、南宋理宗皇帝手书的走马塘宗祠“遗忠堂”匾额、民国“紫来桥”桥匾等，如今都在馆里得到妥善保护。小小的展馆继承着古村重学、重孝、重廉的传统和耕读文化铸就的气节。

夕阳西下时离开走马塘村，霞光满天，古村依旧宁静、祥和。余晖映照下的河面水波盈盈，树冠迎风摇曳。1000 年来，风雨卷走的是岁月沧桑，沉淀下来的是人文醇香。

Zoumatang Village

Zhejiang Province, an eastern coastal province in China, has been a propitious place since ancient times for producing great minds and precious treasures. Picking lotus seeds, washing yarn, drinking plum wine, and reading thread-bound Chinese books are all favorite activities for residents there, displaying picturesque Jiangnan (a nickname for the region south of the Yangtze River) with many legends and stories of talented men and beautiful ladies one generation after another. Zoumatang Village is one of the representatives of the scenes of Chinese Jiangnan. Located in Jiangshan Town, Yinzhou District, Ningbo City, and within the Yinnan plain in the east of Zhejiang Province, this ancient village has a profound history and cultural background, with honest and unsophisticated residents as well as a large number of historic buildings established in Ming and Qing Dynasties. What is more splendid is that this village teemed with scholars and officials in feudal China, with a total of 76 *Jinshi* (graduates who passed the triennial court exam in the Imperial Examination), 111 graduates from *Guozijian* (the Imperial College), and 155 state and local officials in the past dynasties, leaving the village a legend of each family having scholars and officials for many generations and the fame of "the most famous village in China for numerous scholars and officials". This place is also praised as an ancient village full of literary achievements, with fertile land and gorgeous scenery. Zoumatang Village now has a population of over 1, 500, all of whom are surnamed Chen.

According to historical documents, the ancient village of Zoumatang was built in 988, during the reign of Emperor Duangong in North Song Dynasty. At that time, Chen Jin, the magistrate of Mingzhou (similar to current Ningbo City) passed away. His son moved near to the graveyard with the whole family to mourn for him, and then developed this area into a small village. The village has already went through 38 generations in over a thousand years, during which period whenever the descendants of Chen family went back home, they should enter the village on foot, with the civil officials getting off their sedan chairs and military officers getting down from the horses. Zoumatang is also named from this custom.

Consisting of two natural villages, Zoumatang has an overall area of around two *square kilometers*, with eight ancient buildings built in Ming Dynasty, a great number of architectures constructed in

^走马塘村入口牌坊

Stone memorial archway at the entrance of Zoumatang

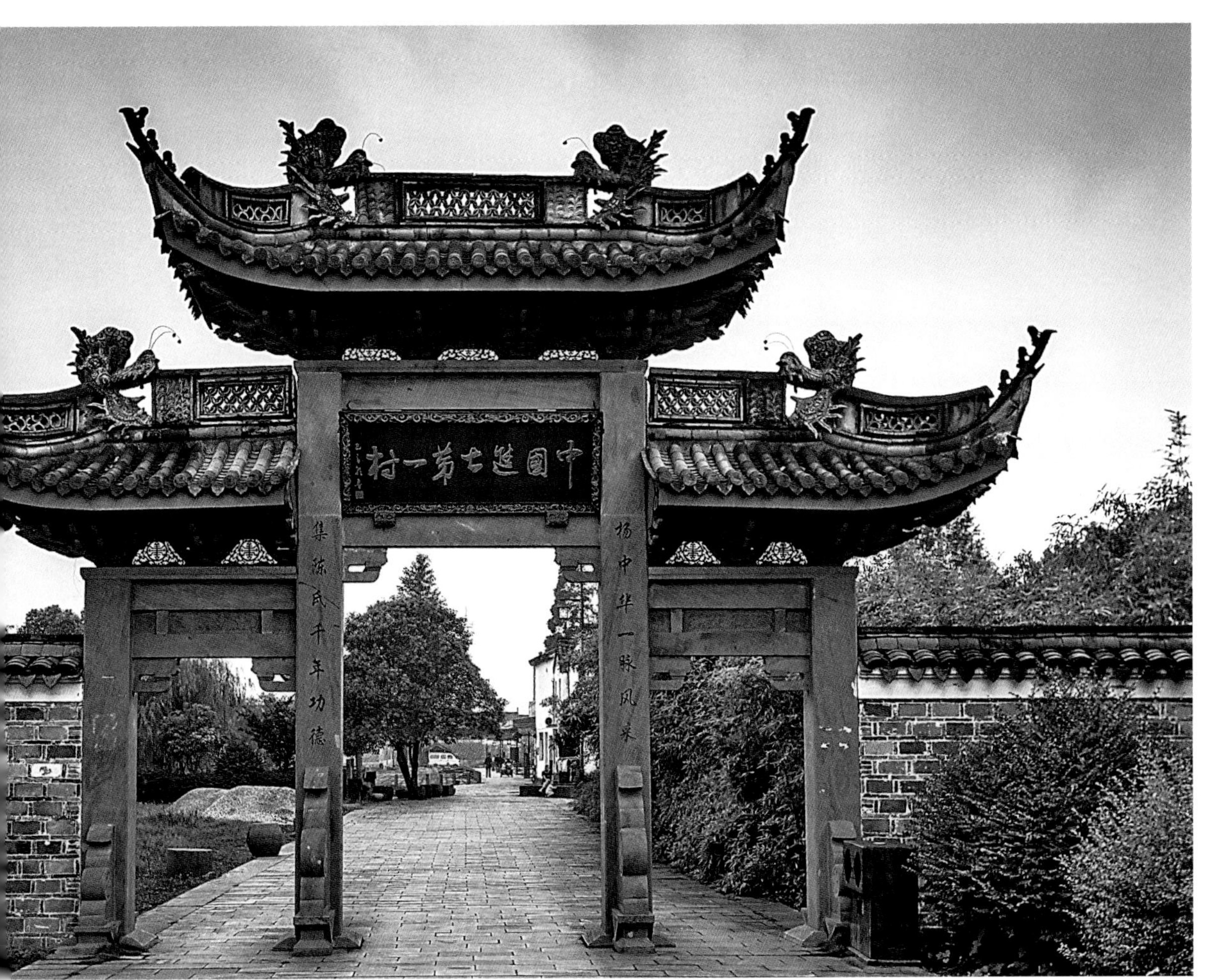

Qing Dynasty, and three western-style buildings established during the period of the Republic of China (1912-1949). Its unique water system is one of the major features of Zoumatang, as this area is surrounded by four rivers with a number of bridges across them, such as Zilaiqiao Bridge, Xishenqiao Bridge and Qingfengqiao Bridge, as well as ponds and water transportation stations like Donglincao, Shaojiacao, Xieduqi, Houwangcao, Xujiacao, and ten or more small ponds scattered in the villages. The well-designed river dredging system can both retain and drain water smoothly to safeguard the village away from drought, flood and conflagration.

As an ancient village giving birth to plenty of successful scholars and officials, Zoumatang Village is supposed to be full of richly ornamented academic mansions coupled with a picturesque landscape and an intelligent atmosphere. However, the village in fact is a simple and rustic area in the countryside which is perhaps not a venue for bustling parties, but a place that needs to be tasted in a quiet stroll by oneself.

^马头墙倒影

Reflection of a horse-head-shaped wall

Entering the stone memorial archway carvin the words "Jin Shi Cun" (village of scholars), and passing through the Zilaiqiao Bridge which was designed and constructed during the period of the Republic of China, visitors will see some ancient dilapidated brick houses telling the story of a long history. In the misty deep and quiet alleys, the upswept eaves of the horse-head-shaped walls seem as if they could thrust the blue sky.

Zhongxinwu Courtyard Complex, the largest architectural complex in the village, is located in the northeastern corner and was built in the reign of Emperor Qianlong of Qing Dynasty. Covering a total area of 4000 *square meters*, this architectural complex has in total 432 houses with five patio for dozens of families to enjoy the sunshine, the gentle breeze and the rain. Many corridors with windows and aisles are vertically and horizontally arranged, enabling the connectivity of all the rooms, and making sure that people do not need to bring umbrellas when walking through this large yard in rainy days. In front of the courtyard, there is a lotus pond larger than 1,300 *square meters*, with two arch bridges across it from north to south. Growing in mud, yet never contaminated by it, the lotus is the flower that represents families in Zoumatang. In every early summer, the lotus blossoms, gracefully erecting in the pond which reflects houses and upturned eaves around it, which forms a vivid scene of a typica water-town in a Chinese fine brushing painting.

The ancient street in Zoumatang is a relatively short one which is only 20 to 30 *mete* long and it was the only passage between Jiangshan Town to Fenghua City in the past. Already well developed during the middle and late Qing Dynasty and running from east to west, this ancient flagged street is around five *meters* wide, with a number of two-storey buildings standing on both sides. Most of the first floors of these buildings are open as shops and the second floors are used for accommodation. In the most prosperous period, when the market was open, boats from other towns crowded in the quay, and streams of people went through the hustle and bustle, buying and selling goods in bundles or piles of various origins, including seafoods from Chunhu Lake in Fenghua City, bamboos from Maoshan Mountain, fish and shrimps from Doumenqiao Village, roots of lotus from Zoumatang and fresh fruits and vegetables from the countryside. Stores selling southern native delicacies, taverns, rice shops, jewelry stores and inns were arranged in close order, rows upon rows. Besides the regular markets, it is particularly lively and boisterous in the village in the Riceflower Festival on every May 25th in Chinese lunar calendar. In that night, each and every family would set an offering table with sacrificial offerings with flickering lights that lit up the whole street.

Along this flagged street, visitors will step into the core area of Zoumatang: the Xieduqi, a small pond connecting inner and outer waters around the village. Ringed on thre sides by stone banks which facilitate people to tie the boat up alongside the quay, this pond also has several stone steps for villagers to wash and brush, and for boatman to get ashore. Reflecting white walls, black tiles and wooden window lattices, the surface of the pond is like a picture itself while women doing laundry break up the pattern occasionally. A millennium-year-old tree stretches over the river with branches like the beard of Chinese dragon (a legendary powerful creature in Chinese mythology and Chinese folklore), and the crown luxuriantly green. It cannot be known the exact reason why this pond was named Xieduqi. However, in Chinese, the name not only means the center of the village and also reflects wishes of people who travel or reside in other places far away from Zoumatang to return home and join the clan again. During the long period in history when the imperial examination system existed in China, plenty of young men embarked here, leaving their home for the capital to attend the examination and realize their dream of glorifying and illuminating the whole family.

To the west of Xieduqi, there stands alone a small courtyard, covered by honeysuckle and other herbs on the door. This courtyard, with the name of Yigutang, is the private clinic of Chen Songtao, a famous doctor who was praised by people as "Demigod Chen" in the south of Yinzhou District during the period of the Republic of China. In Zoumatang, there are three specialties which have been famous for around a century. They are the Clinic Yigutang, the Fire-fighting Equipment which has been donated to relevant departments of Shanghai municipal government, and the Old-style Private School which has been developed into a modern primary school. Only this clinic stands unchanged at all. Entering the clinic, people will notice a large round ancient coin engraved in the ground, with a blooming white lotus in the middle of it to symbolize the unsullied and decent personality of Doctor Chen. Flowers, trees and other plants for all seasons grow in the yard, leaving pleasant aroma even in the clothes of passers-by.

Taking a detour around the ancestral shrine of the the Chen family in the southwest corner of the village, visitors can see a clear river named the River of Noble Man meandering before their eyes. There is an old saying that even the willow trees around the Pond of Gentleman is gentle, and the flowers along the River of Noble Man are noble. Being both farmers and scholars for generations, all members of the Chen family lived and worked based on the moral family tradition to do what noble men would do, and the characters of "Noble Man" elaborate the expectations of Chens' ancestors for their descendants. In the eighth year of the reign of Emperor Jiayou of the North Song Dynasty (1063), Chen Mi, the former vice-minister of the Libu Department, a major department in ancient China in charge of officers' appointments and dismissals, resigned from his office and took a little boat drifting thousands of miles to return to Zoumatang. The villagers lined along the banks to welcome him, and saw two heavy wooden boxes being lifted ashore. At first they thought that the boxes would be full of silver ingots, but it turned out to be two boxes of books that seemed somewhat worn because of frequent reading. His story and the good reputation flowed down for ages. Influenced by a rich cultural atmosphere in the village, members of the Chen family have been building up the whole family based on the farming-reading culture to achieve the ambition of seeking knowledge consistently and being intellectuals for thousands of years without any break.

On the east wall of the house in the north of the ancestral shrine, there appears an exquisite stone window which is specially named by scholars as the "Representative of Stone Window in Southern Zhejiang Province". On this window, visitors could find various patterns related to exorcising evil spirits, wishing for peace and fortune and praying for luck and happiness, including figures like Zhang Guolao, Lan Caihe and Lü Dongbin (all of which are Chinese mythological figures of the Eight Immortals in the Taoist pantheon), and the characters such as "Fu" and "Qian" (auspicious words in Chinese). Being detailedly carved, this hollow-out stone window is not only classic and unsophisticated, but can also be closed and opened as smoothly as a wooden window. Overhanging eaves accompanied

∨民居柱式

Columns of a dwelling

with carved beams and painted rafters are the common sights around. One of the most magnificent horse-head-shaped walls here is the one with five corbiesteps going up by degrees one after another with exquisitely carved patterns. Due to rigid stratification in Ming and Qing Dynasties, only the residence of government officials could be decorated like this.

Besides all the above mentioned splendid buildings, there is also a private archive in Zoumatang, preserving over ten thousand copies of valuable materials about this village, including but not limited to calligraphy and paintings, photographs, newspapers, books and plaques. The owner of this archive is not one of the descendants of the Chen family, but an educated Chinese citizen who came here when he was young during the Culture Revolution when millions of the city-bred educated youths across China settled in the countryside and merged with the peasants to farm for a living. However, when he was back home, he still kept Zoumatang in his mind and carried it away in his dreams for many years. Therefore, he returned his second home in 2005 and spared no effort to collect documents and cultural relics related to the village. His collections include art works themed with the village by calligraphers and painters throughout the country, and portraits of the 76 *Jinshi* painted by famous artists. Furthermore, the horizontal inscribed board with the Chinese characters of "The First Mountain in the South" from Pu'an Temple which has been around for over a thousand years, the "Yi Zhong Tang" board of the ancestral shrine in Zoumatang which bears the calligraphy of Emperor Lizong in the Southern Song Dynasty, as well as the board of Zilaiqiao Bridge which was established in the Republican period of China are also well kept here. This archive, though small in size, provides the collections with safekeeping and exhibits the village's tradition of attaching great importance to knowledge, filial piety and probity.

We left Zoumatang when the sun was sinking in the west. Bathing in the evening twilight, this ancient village looks peaceful and quiet, with the river reflecting the last radiance of the setting sun on its glistening water and the crown of trees dancing in the breeze. Over a thousand years, all the twists and turns of life have gone with the wind and the rain, leaving only profound cultural deposits and rich spiritual treasures.

^ 老街

An ancient street

> 马头墙局部

Part of a horse-head-shaped wall

∨前兴屋与荷花池

Qianxingwu
Courtyard
Complex and the
Lotus pond

^遗忠塘内部

Indoor settings of Yizhongtang

> 前兴屋

Qianxingwu House

10

佛寺村

调查报告原文 / 摄影
关秀峰

Reported / photograghed by
Guan Xiufeng

> 晨雾中放羊

Pasturing sheep in the morning mist

雪域梵音传辽西

一座完整的古村至少包含 3 个方面：首先是完整的村貌、原生态的环境和传统建筑；其次是独具色的传承着源远流长文化底蕴的非物质文化遗产，如技艺、民俗、艺术；最后是具有传统文化美德的朴民风。按照这个标准，辽宁省阜新市蒙古族自治县佛寺镇佛寺村就是一处保存完好的传统村落。这历史遗迹星罗棋布，自然景观令人赞叹，还蕴藏着神秘的“东藏”文化。作为蒙古族人的聚居地，还是力格尔（俗称蒙古琴书）的故乡，有民族美食喇嘛炖肉、蒙古馅饼、手扒羊肉等，集自然风光、宗教文民俗民风为一体。

佛寺村三面环山，伊玛图河自东北向西南从村前流过，镇政府与各个行政村间均有公路相通，交便利。不远处的佛寺水库水域宽阔，是避暑的好去处，这里还是辽宁省体育局皮划艇训练基地。

走进村庄，迎面便是一座大气雄浑的藏传佛教寺庙。寺庙香火鼎盛，在蓝天白云下金碧辉煌，宛

小版的布达拉宫，这就是瑞应寺。佛寺村就是伴随着这座名寺而兴起的。如今全村 1200 多人，中蒙古族占 90% 以上。

当地人称瑞应寺为葛根苏木，俗称佛爷喇嘛寺，简称佛寺。背靠巍巍的阿贵山，东临蜿蜒伏的白音花山，西接查干哈达山，东西两座山脉如同大鹏展翅，护住佛寺。清澈的泉水从西脚下流向东南，与伊玛图河汇流到一起。一世活佛修行过的地方——哈达山，巍然耸立在东南，色宜人的平坦大地上，殿宇佛塔峥嵘，松柏檀香翠绿，这里是东北地区的藏传佛教中心，演着让人无限向往的雪域风情。

寺内的金瓦殿是目前东北及内蒙古地区唯一的金瓦殿，耗用千足黄金 20 余千克。庙顶的瓦和大殿内的铜佛像全部由当地工匠以传统手艺镏金制成。大殿内主供一尊 13 米高的铜质镏金弥勒佛，还有 4 口超大口径的镏金大铜锅，堪称天下无双。

瑞应寺始建于清康熙八年(1669 年)。时值第一世活佛桑丹桑布四处寻觅建庙地址，行至佛寺镇时，他发现这里三面环山，呈面南背北的坐骑状分布，平地开阔，祥云朵朵，万物茂盛，是一方宝地。于是，他奏请康熙皇帝恩准，便在这里修建寺庙、传经布道。康熙皇帝赐名、题字匾额，将桑丹桑布活佛赐名为大清东部蒙古老佛爷。

佛寺开工后，集万千能工巧匠之技，仿西藏布达拉宫之势，历时 200 多年，多次扩建。方圆十里山谷中，钟鼓和鸣，禅境幽远，红墙碧瓦，廊檐高耸。道光年间，寺院达到鼎盛，形成了气势恢宏的佛教建筑群，真是“有名喇嘛三千六，没名喇嘛赛牛毛”。

瑞应寺历世活佛都受到皇帝的礼遇，他们年年进京为皇帝诵经祈福。平时也法事频繁，每年还会举行 8 ~ 9 次大型法会，包括盛大的查玛(金刚驱魔法舞)舞会。法会期间，四面八方的蒙古族群众云集，是草原上盛大的节日。

瑞应寺的喇嘛多是蒙古族饱学之士，这里先后走出了一大批医药、哲学、历法学方面的学者，堪称培养精英的摇篮，对蒙古族文化艺术的发展产生了深远影响。受佛寺熏陶，佛寺村也是人文鼎盛之地，是蒙古文化奇葩——安代舞和经箱乐的发源地。

古老的村落一片祥和，僧俗相处融洽。村民信仰佛教，遇到大小事情经常请喇嘛念经开示，尤其是活佛在当地享有崇高的地位。

村民热情好客，讲究礼仪。骑马或坐车路遇必先下马或下车请安，男女老幼尊卑有序。当有远方的客人光临时，哈达是最圣洁、最崇高的吉祥物。村民用双手将哈达举过头顶向客人敬献的传统流传至今。蒙古族人喜欢喝茶，客人登门拜访，主人先以茶待客。蒙古馅饼是本村久负盛名的风味食品，同样出名的还有喇嘛炖肉——用新鲜的猪肉和咸白菜加上各种特色调味品慢火炖熟，食之齿颊留香，是欢庆节日或招待贵宾的佳品。酒过三巡，蒙古汉子开始饮酒高歌，露出热情豪爽的真性情。在节日之时，家家户户更是欢声一片。

佛寺村的街道呈东西走向，俗称胡同。如今村里依然保留着原有的 13 条胡同的格局。村子最南端的胡同叫买卖胡同，现在成了集贸市场；村南的第二条胡同即章楚衮地胡同，是蒙医鼻祖章楚衮地喇嘛的故居所在地。有趣的是，村里还有裤裆胡同、灰堆胡同、接生胡同……其中以万佛路北的弥勒胡同最具风情。胡同里的瓦房墙壁上的砖雕精巧别致，居室窗前的吉祥结与窗台上的虎头装饰不怒自威。在蒙古族传统里，13 是个吉祥数字，因而村落的胡同建了 13 条。此外，村里的 13 个大碾子、13 盘大磨等也遵循这个传统。碾子石磨还有更深的寓意：碾子石磨为石材，但是它再硬也有轴心。没有轴心的话，便不能发挥作用。这是用实物来教育村里人——人再强壮也得有心，离德离心不行。佛寺村周围环绕的三山、三泉、三坡、四沟，不仅赋予这片土地神秘和神圣感，它们加在一起也正好是 13。四沟的命名充满了人情味。比如其中的翁沁沟又称姐姐沟，是一条生长着 100 多种草药的沟壑，植被繁茂，是传说中金马驹的吃草之地。乌达木头沟又称妹妹沟，此沟曾住有一位高僧——瑞应寺七世活佛，沟里有

> 佛寺村有一条通往山上的正在修建的十轮金刚塔的路，路边竖着一块大石头，上面用汉蒙两种文字刻着万佛路

Wanfo Road is leading up to the mountain where the Shilun Kingkong Tower (under construction) is located. The name "Wanfo Road" is being engraved on a rock in both Chinese and Mongolian characters

块长约 35 米，宽 15 米，高 4 米的黄色方石，据说这是庙的装钱柜。此外，还有母亲沟、姑姑沟。

作为拥有数百年历史的古村，在这里还能见到保存好的沙影太房（即蒙古传统民居）。以前，人们这样形佛寺村村民的生活状态，“前出狼牙，后出稍。两道大一口井，细米干柴三间房”。现存的沙影太虽然经历了雨沧桑，仍能从中窥见过去的风貌和手工技艺。

沙影太都有正房三间，耳房两厢，还有两道门。其饰非常讲究，砖雕、石雕、木雕的飞禽走兽、花鸟虫鱼栩如生，吉祥图案也描绘细致。门口有三级或五级台，石兽礅子威严肃穆。走下二门台阶便进入院落，院西一般种有藏红花，东侧种玉簪花，石雕花坛古朴端庄。往里走约 30 步便可踏上正房石阶，房梁为四梁八柱，梁两端设有凹陷处，用来装元宝和古钱。主檩下方还悬挂一双乌木筷子和一个紫色口袋，内装五谷种子。

有趣的是，房间东、西、后墙内侧用土坯筑成，便于挖开做壁龛，悬挂佛像，供神祭祖。还能保温防风，冬暖夏凉。墙体外侧用石料垒砌，并用石灰勾缝，坚固朴实。房子多为口袋房，屋门设在东面或西面。也有少数钱褡房，从中间开门。

蒙古族风情佛教文化和东北乡情在佛寺村完美融合。从佛寺村走出，穿街走巷，沐浴着金黄的夕阳余晖，信步爬上附近的山坡俯瞰村庄，躺在脚下的村子仿佛是一块蒙古族的传统吉祥图案。没错，300 多年前，佛寺村祖先就是这样煞费苦心地规划村庄的布局，希望子子孙孙吉祥如意。果然，300 多年后，这个古老的村落仍然兴旺发达，成为著名的文化旅游交流中心。

Fosi Village

An ancient village contains at least three aspects: first, the appearance of the village shall remain intact with an original ecological environment and traditional architectures; second, the village shall possess profound cultural foundations and be distinctive with a variety of intangible cultural heritages such as crafts, folklore and art which can be traced back to the earliest days; third, traditional virtues shall be manifested in an unsophisticated folkway. According to the above standard, Fosi Village, located in Fumeng County, Fuxin City, Liaoning Province can be reputed as a complete traditional village. In Fosi Village, there are many historical heritages, stunning natural sceneries and the mysterious "Eastern Tibetan" culture. Inhabited by Mongolians, Fosi Village is also the origin of the Mongol vocal art form "*Wuligeer*" (literally means story telling) and has various delicacies such as "Lama Style Pork Stew", "Mongol Meat Pie" and "Hand-grabbed Mutton". So to speak, there is a mixture of natural sceneries, religious cultures and folk customs in Fosi village.

Fosi Village is surrounded by mountains on three sides in the east, west and north, and in front of the village lies the Yimatu River, rippling from northeast to southwest. Despite that, Fosi Village connects to other administrativevillages with a convenient highway network. Not far away is a large reservoir in Fosi Village, which is a good summer resort with a fresh breeze sweeping through and also a kayak training base of the Liaoning Province Sports Bureau of Liaoning Province.

Upon entrance to the village, a magnificent Tibetan Buddhist Temple appears. Glittering under blue sky and white clouds, this popular temple resembles a smaller version of Potala Palace. It is called the Ruiying Temple, and Fosi Village emerged along with the thriving of this Tibetan Buddhist temple. Currently, Fosi Village has a population of over 1,200, with Mongolian residents accounting for more than 90%.

Mongolians call the Ruiying Temple "Ge gen su mu" (a Mongolian pronunciation, which means Buddhist temple) and it is also known as "Buddhist Lama Temple" or simply "Buddhist Temple". Fosi Village is backed against the majestic Mt. A Gui, with the winding and tortuous Mt. Baiyinhua to the east and Mt. Chagan hada to the west. Those two mountains in the east and west look like two spread wings of a hawk, protecting the Buddhist Temple. Clear springs flow from the mountain foot in the west to the southeast, and converge at the Yimatu River. Besides, Mt. Hada, where a Living Buddha "Yishi" once lived his ascetic life, stands erect in the southeast. With its picturesque sceneries, lush pines, cypresses and sandalwoods and lofty palaces and temples around, this place became the center of Tibetan Buddhism in northeast China, displaying a flavor of infinite yearning.

^赶集的喇嘛

A lama at a fair

Inside the Ruiying Temple, there is a Jinwa Hall that consumed more than 20 *kilogram* pure gold (24 *karal* gold) in construction, making it the one and only gold tile hall in the Northeast and Inner Mongolian area at present. Both the gold tiles of the temple roof and the bronze Buddha statue standing in the main hall were made by Tibetan Buddhist artisans with a traditional skill—gold gilding. In the main hall stands Buddha Maitreya (a symbol of a bright future), a bronze gold-gilding Buddha statue with 13 *meters* in height, long hands (1.3 *meters*) and big ears (1.1 *meters* high). Besides, the four large bronze pots with extra-long diameters in the main hall are considered to be unmatched in the world.

The erection of Ruiying Temple dates back to the eighth year under the reign of Emperor Kangxi in the Qing Dynasty (1699). It is said that the first generation of Living Buddha called Sangdansangbu searched in vain for a perfect place to build a temple until he arrived at Fosi Village. He found that this place was surrounded by mountains on three sides, backing against the north and facing the south, and thought it was a precious land full of vigor and prosperity. Therefore, with the assent of Emperor Kangxi, the temple was built and he began his preaching. Furthermore, Emperor Kangxi granted a plaque to Ruiying Temple and also bestowed a name to the Living Buddha Sangdansangbu as the "Old Buddha in Eastern Mongolia during the tine of the Great Qing Dynasty".

The temple was constructed by tens of thousands of skilled craftsmen and its appearance resembled the Potala Palace in Tibet. It took more than 200 years to complete the construction, including several expansions. With red walls, green tiles, high eaves and the resonance of bells, the temple and even the ten *mile* radius around it

< 蒙古族的酒盅舞

Mongol Wine-cup Dance

were filled with a buddhist atmosphere. Under the reign of Emperor Daoguang, the temple culture reached its heyday and the country witnessed a surge in grand Buddhist temples. At that time, there was a saying to describe the large number of lamas of Ruiying Temple: "famous Lamas are over three thousand while ordinary lamas are countless within".

Generations after generations, Living Buddhas in the Ruiying Temple were treated with the utmost courtesy by emperors and they would travel to the capital and pray blessings for the emperors every year. Lamas were quite busy with frequent religious rituals in their daily life, not to mention the large-scale buddhist ceremonies that would be held eight to nine times annually, including the grand "Chama" dance ceremony (for expelling devils). Crowds of Mongolians from all directions would gather together for the ceremonies, the grandest occasions in the vast grassland.

In the Ruiying Temple, most lamas were well-educated Mongolians and successors to *lama* scholars in medicine, philosophy, astronomy and calendric studies who made eminent achievements, which made the Ruiying Temple a cradle of elites, exerting profound and lasting effects onthe development of Mongolian art. Under the influence of the Ruiying Temple, Fosi Village witnessed a thriving of extraordinary cultures, and was the origin place of Mongolian cultural wonders, such as the "Andai" dance (reputed as a living fossil of Mongolian dance) and "Jingxiang" music (also called temple music, an instrumental music form of Mongolian Buddhism). Lamas and the ordinary villagers get along with each other peacefully in this ancient village. As being sincere is a Buddhist belief, villagers have especially high reverence for the Living Buddhas and will invite lamas to chant prayers and give advice when confronted with troubles, big or small.

Being friendly and hospitable, the locals also lay emphasis on manners. When passing each other, those who ride or drive will dismount and greet each other sincerely in an orderly manner (being noble or humble, man or woman, young or old). For the guests coming from afar, *hada* (a white silk scarf) will be presented with both hands, held up higher than the head. Hada presentation is considered to be the holiest and most noble etiquette in Mongolian culture and has passed on from generation to generation until today. When calling on Mongolians, the guests will be first entertained with tea by the host as Mongolians like drinking tea. Besides, there are typical Mongolian foods such as "Mongolian Meat Pie", a well-known specialty in Fosi Village and "Lama Style Pork Stew", a stewed dish made with pork and cabbages, accompanied by special flavorings, which serve for holiday occasions and distinguished guests. At banquets, Mongolian men will be in high spirits and begin to drink and sing, demonstrating their passionate and vigorous nature. Especially at holidays, every household will be filled with laughter and cheers.

Running from east to west, the roads in Fosi Village are often called "*hutong*" and 13 *hutongs* still remain in the village today. The southernmost *hutong* is called Maimai Hutong (meaning doing business) and now it has become a township trade market. The second *hutong* in the south is Zhangchugundi Hutong, the former residence of Lama Zhangchugundi, the master and founder of Mongolian medicine. The names of the *hutongs* are interesting such as "Kudang" (meaning the crotch of trousers), "Huidui" (meaning a pile of ashes), and "Jiesheng" (meaning delivering a baby). The Maitreya *hutong* in Wanfo North Road is of great aesthetic taste that can be seen in its delicate brick carvings on the walls, the auspicious knots in the front of the windows and the awesome ornaments— tiger heads at the window sills. Villagers said that "13" is an auspicious number in Mongolian tradition and that is why there are 13 *hutongs* in the village. Additionally, the village also has exactly 13 stone rollers and 13 stone mills. Regarding the rollers and mills, there is a deeper connotation: though being made of hard stones, the rollers and mills all have an axis. Without an axis, they wouldn't be able to function properly. This illustrates a principle that no matter how powerful and strong one may become, one shall adhere to virtues and morals in life.

Surrounded by three mountains, three springs, three hillsides and four hollows, this piece of land is full of mystery and sacred spirits. Coincidently enough, by adding up these landmarks, the total is also "13". The names of the four hollows are also interesting and have extra meanings. For example, the "Wengqin" Hollow, also called "Jiejie" Hollow (which means elder sister), is a hollow fostering more than 100 herbs and having luxuriant vegetation. Local legend has it that Gold Horses once came here and grazed on it. "Wudamutou" Hollow, also called "Meimei" Hollow (which means younger sister), once had an eminent monk—the seventh generation of a Living Buddha in the Ruiying

Temple. Besides, a yellowish square stone lies in this hollow 35 *meters* in length, 15 *meters* in width and 4 *meters* in height .It is said to be the money till of the temple. The other two hollows are nicknamed "Mama" (which means mother) and "Gugu" (which means aunt).

In this ancient village with several hundred years of history, "shayingtai" houses, i.e. Mongol traditional residences can still be seen in good condition. In the old days, people described the typical architectural structures and the real life of villagers in Fosi Village as follows: with wide eaves in the front and at the back, two entrances and one well in the house, villagers live a simple life with basic daily needs. Through the vicissitude of time, the existing "shayingtai" houses are still relatively well preserved so people can still have a glimpse of the appearance and craftwork in the old days.

"Shayingtai" homes have three principal rooms: two penthouses and two entrances. The the exquisite decorations of the house can be witnessed in the remarkable craftwork (brick carvings, stone carvings and wood carvings) with all kinds of birds, beasts, flowers and fishes engraved on them as well as delicate auspicious patterns. At the entrance, there are three or five staircases with two solemn stone beasts at each side. Walking inside the second entrance, there will be a courtyard with saffrons growing in the west side and hostas (funkia plantain lily) in the east side. The stone-carved flowerbed in the courtyard also displays a sense of simplicity and delicacy. Walking another 30 steps, one will reach a principal room. Looking up at the roof, one will find four large beams supported by eight columns (a typical structure in wooden architecture). At both ends of the main beam, there are cavities for storing ancient ingots and coins. Under the main beam hang a pair of ebony chopsticks and a purple bag with some grain seeds (rice, wheat, soy bean, corn and potato) inside.

Interestingly, the internal walls are covered with a layer of clay for the convenience of digging niches, where the Buddha statues or ancestors' memorial tablets will be put. Additionally, the clay also helps guard against strong winds in winter. The external walls are built with stone materials, which guarantee the house can stand firm for years. Most of the rooms are like "pockets" with the doors only open at one side, either in the east or in the west while a few rooms with archways open in the middle.

Fosi Village has a perfect combination of Mongolian tastes, Buddhist cultures and northeast customs. Walking out of the temple and climbing up a nearby hillside, one will find that Fosi Village is shaped like the "Wuliji", an auspicious knot in the Mongol tradition. Surprisingly, back to three hundred years ago, the ancestors of Fosi Village took great pains to plan the layout of the village in the hope of bringing blessings and fortunes to their offspring. As expected, this ancient village still flourishes three hundred years later and is now reputed to be an exchange center of cultural tourism.

^ 关帝庙内——关帝庙是为了供奉三国时期蜀国的大将关羽而建

Inside the Guandi Temple, a temple dedicated to Guan Yu,a heroic General of Shu Kingdom during the Three Kingdoms period

^早上，一位蒙古族老者推着自行车送孙子去上学

In the morning, an elderly Mongolian sent his grandson to kindergarten by bike

^ 一个骑着摩托车的汉子，车后面装满农家土鸡，去瑞应寺广场赶集

Carrying a full basket of hens, a man on a motorcycle was going to a fair at the Ruiying Temple square

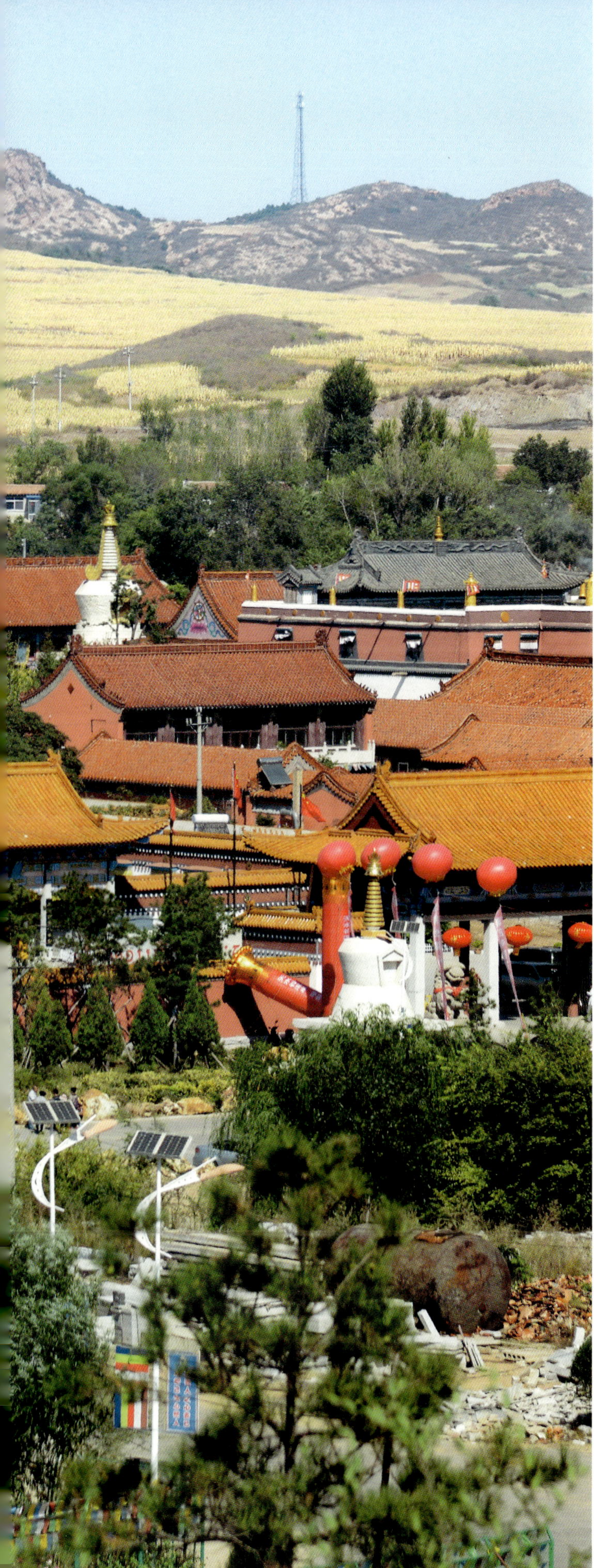

< 瑞应寺长寿宫开光庆典

Opening ceremony of Changshou Palace in the Ruiying Temple

图书在版编目(CIP)数据

乡愁·中国. 卷壹 : 汉、英 / 《乡愁·中国》编委会编 ; 李谨羽译. — 北京 : 北京出版社，2016.9
ISBN 978-7-200-12211-4

Ⅰ. ①乡… Ⅱ. ①乡… ②李… Ⅲ. ①村落 — 调查报告 — 中国 — 汉、英 Ⅳ. ① K928.5

中国版本图书馆 CIP 数据核字 (2016) 第 121452 号

选题策划：孙　宇
责任编辑：孙　宇
执行编辑：李姝惠
英文审校：王若凡　贾婉玲
责任校对：魏旭辉
责任印制：魏　鹏
书籍设计：刘晓翔工作室　刘晓翔　范美玲

乡愁 · 中国　卷壹　汉、英
XIANGCHOU · ZHONGGUO　JUAN YI　HAN、YING
《乡愁 · 中国》编委会　编　李谨羽　译

出　　版：北京出版集团公司
　　　　　北京出版社
地　　址：北京北三环中路 6 号
邮　　编：100120
网　　址：www.bph.com.cn
总 发 行：北京出版集团公司
版　　次：2016 年 9 月第 1 版第 1 次印刷
印　　刷：北京顺诚彩色印刷有限公司
开　　本：787 毫米 ×1092 毫米　1/16
印　　张：12.25
字　　数：240 千字
书　　号：ISBN 978-7-200-12211-4
定　　价：98.00 元
质量监督电话：010 – 58572393